THE PEOPLE'S LAWYER

THE PEOPLE'S LAWYER

The Center for Constitutional Rights and the Fight for Social Justice, from Civil Rights to Guantánamo

by ALBERT RUBEN

MONTHLY REVIEW PRESS
New York

Copyright © 2011 by Albert Ruben
All rights reserved

Library of Congress Cataloging-in-Publication Data
Ruben, Albert.
The people's lawyer : the Center for Constitutional Rights and the fight for social justice, from civil rights to Guantánamo, / by Albert Ruben.
p. cm.
ISBN 978-1-58367-237-2 (pbk.) — ISBN 978-1-58367-238-9 (cloth) 1. Center for Constitutional Rights (New York, N.Y.) 2. Civil rights—United States. 3. Public interest law—United States. 4. Human rights advocacy—United States. I. Title.
KF4749.R83 2011
342.7308'5—dc22

2011007669

Monthly Review Press
146 West 29th Street, Suite 6W
New York, NY 10001
www.monthlyreview.org

5 4 3 2 1

Contents

For Martha
Julie
David and Nancy
and for Judy

~

Are we going to accept despair, without doing anything?
I suppose that no one honest can answer yes.
—Albert Camus

CHAPTER 1

You Have the Body

He held up for traffic at the corner of Bond Street and Broadway in lower Manhattan on a May day in 2009. His cell phone vibrated in his jacket pocket. The caller wanted to know if he could be at the White House at 10:45 the next morning for a meeting with the president. He stalled. He hates to be hustled, and his immediate take was that the Obama administration wanted, if not to win his organization's active support for the government's Guantánamo policies, to at least blunt its criticisms and provide the administration with tacit cover. Vincent Warren told the caller he'd be there.

Gathered in the cabinet room of the West Wing were the executive directors of the American Civil Liberties Union, Human Rights Watch, and Warren of the Center for Constitutional Rights, and an associate director of the Center for American Progress. The president's team was composed of Chief of Staff Rahm Emanuel, Attorney General Eric Holder, Senior Advisor David Axelrod, Presidential Assistant Valerie Jarrett, and White House Counsel Gregory Craig. President Obama did the talking. Warren says Obama asked that the substance of the meeting be kept off the record. Warren also says he quickly understood that the president's reason for calling the meeting was to lay out his government's rationale for the procedures it would follow in closing the detention center at the Guantánamo Bay Naval Station in Cuba. While Cuba technically retains sovereignty, the naval base at the southeast end of Cuba has been under the "complete jurisdiction and control" of the United States since the Cuban-American Treaty following the Spanish-American War. The United States pays an annual rent. Since the revolution, the Cuban government hasn't cashed the checks.

The sense Warren drew from the president's remarks was that the U.S. government was trying to find a middle ground in its Guantánamo policies between what is legal and what isn't. As far as the Center for Constitutional Rights (CCR) is concerned, no such middle ground exists.

The Center is a not-for-profit law office dedicated to using the law creatively to effect social change and to advance and defend rights guaranteed by the Universal Declaration of Human Rights. Its efforts to make sure marginalized communities are entitled to justice, as well as its strong educational component, are features that set it apart from conventional civil liberties organizations.

Warren takes his presence at the White House that day for granted: any convocation of A-list civil rights organizations would almost by definition include the CCR. Not many years before his tenure began in 2006, however, he would not have been able to make the same assumption. September 11, 2001 set in motion a series of events that brought about a dramatic change in the Center's fortunes.

Two months after the World Trade Center attacks, President George W. Bush, in his role as Commander in Chief and as a stratagem in his recently declared war on terror, issued Military Order Number One. Under the order, the government could capture non-U.S. citizens (it was later amended to include citizens) thought to be involved in international terrorism anywhere in the world. Anyone arrested under the order could be held indefinitely without charge. If charges were filed, trials would be before an ad hoc "military commission." The proceedings would be held in secret, and those found guilty could be executed in secret. Finally, no court was to be allowed to hear any appeal from any person detained under the order. In other words, Bush was suspending the right to *habeas corpus*, literally "you have the body." The right was set down by an act of Parliament in 1679 and passed along to the colonies as common law until it was enshrined in Article 1 of the Constitution. The practical effect of the right of *habeas corpus* is that anybody, citizen or alien, who is arrested and held by an agency of government, must be allowed to petition a court of law to challenge his or her detention.

The order's abuse of the U.S. president's constitutional authority was so great, CCR president Michael Ratner recalls, ". . . shock as I read the order. I remember thinking that there has just been a *coup d'état* in America."* Ratner considered the attacks on the Twin Towers to be crimes. Terrible crimes.

*Unless clearly referenced, all quotations throughout this work are from interviews by the author.

Extraordinary crimes. But nonetheless, by definition, criminal acts. If the people who helped commit them were identified and arrested, there were adequate laws to charge them with and federal courts to try them. Ratner was convinced that by arbitrarily declaring a category of crime to be outside the normal judicial process, Bush had usurped power. Something had to be done, an assault launched against the legality of the order. Ratner had a weapon:

> the CCR, a group with only twenty staff members, including lawyers, management, and legal workers. Still, despite its small size and perpetual underfunding, it had, in its thirty-five-year history, in, for example, the South in the Sixties, and in the Vietnam war years, forced giant adversaries to defend themselves. Could this be such a time?

Traditionally, the CCR represents clients with whom it identifies politically. It allies itself with people engaged in social justice activities and encourages them to turn to the courts to advance their causes. In that respect, it's different from the American Civil Liberties Union (ACLU), for example. The group had no quarrel with the ACLU's First Amendment defense of the Nazi Party's right to hold a march in Skokie, Illinois, in 1977, but representing neo-Nazis would have been inconsistent with the CCR's mission. How then could representing people caught up in Bush's order be justified in the event those people turned out to be religious fanatics?

When Bush's military order was being debated, Ratner told me, "I circulated two pages from Bill's [Kunstler] autobiography about the jogger case to say, 'This is a mistake we do not want to make again.'" Defense attorney William M.

Kunstler, a Center founder notorious for taking controversial clients, brought in the highly charged Central Park jogger case for CCR acceptance in 1990, only to be turned aside. The case fit classic civil rights dimensions: five black and Latino teenagers were accused of attacking and raping a young white woman in New York City's Central Park on April 19, 1989, found guilty, and given long prison sentences.

The Center's position at the time was that criminal law did not fit comfortably with its mission. Kunstler nevertheless took on the appeal of Yusef Salaam, one of the five boys convicted largely on the basis of confessions that were later recanted. His spirited efforts to free his client not only failed but drew a contempt-of-court citation. The Center wouldn't even represent Kunstler on the contempt charge. Twelve years later, the sentences were vacated when a prisoner admitted he'd been the attacker, and DNA tests proved the convicted boys, grown men by that time, could not have committed the crime. Thus Kunstler, who died in 1995, was posthumously vindicated.

Morton Stavis, another Center founder, had a similar experience when he brought the Kelly Michaels case before the Center in 1989, only to be rejected. Michaels had been convicted in 1985 of child molestation while a teacher at a New Jersey daycare center. Stavis was convinced of Michaels's innocence. He argued her appeal without help from the CCR, and Michaels was exonerated. Ratner says he never understood why Stavis was rebuffed by his colleagues, given that the child abuse hysteria sweeping the country at the time urgently needed to be confronted.

CCR staffers with long memories bring the chagrin attached to the Michaels and Central Park jogger cases to the process when cases are proposed for Center acceptance.

Ratner hoped those memories were making old-timers uneasy as they weighed going to battle with the government over its Guantánamo policies.

Another consideration was one faced many times at the CCR over the years: did they have a chance of winning? It was a question to which other lawyers invariably added another: wouldn't a loss set a bad precedent? "While the CCR carefully examines the law, it will still bring a case that might not prevail," Ratner explains. "If we have a decent argument, if the client needs representation, and if the case is politically important, we will go ahead. We believe that law, lawsuits, and court hearings have a public education and fight-back dimension that can aid in social struggles and struggles to protect fundamental rights." Everything leading up to a verdict—educating the plaintiffs/defendants, empowering them, educating the public—is as important as the verdict itself.

A big question, too, was what effect taking on the government at a time when emotions were running so high would have on funding. The Center always lived hand-to-mouth. If it got a little ahead, it hired more staff in order to take on more cases or simply to help it do a better job with the ones already on its docket. In the autumn of 2001, more than half the annual budget was raised from individual donors. How many of them, given the country's widespread alarm and vengeful mood, would stop contributing? What about money from foundation grants; would these sources dry up?

While the group struggled with their problem, out in the world their hand was being forced: suspects had begun to be detained under the president's order. And so, without a client, the Center went public with its determination to challenge the order. Angry letters and e-mail messages, some of them threatening, promptly flooded the office. As confirmation of the CCR's fears, several foundations that had been major supporters locked their coffers.

It had been a tough call. After all the discussion, the consensus among the staff was that if and when they have a client, the principle they'll be defending will very likely have little to do with the client's beliefs but will focus on the right of any accused to a process of law defined not by the president but by the Constitution. Ratner says, "*habeas corpus* is the dividing line between a democracy under law and a police state." Staff attorney Shayana Kadidal remembers thinking when the intense debates were done that "this is the kind of commitment you make that you feel is effectively career-ending." Gitanjali Gutierrez, a central member of the Center's Guantánamo Global Justice Initiative, wasn't yet at the Center but remembers her reaction to the news: "From my perspective as an outsider, that was a very brave thing for an organization to do. Many civil liberties organizations are not willing to do it."

When asked by *The New York Times* why the Center would try to limit the president's ability to conduct his war on terror, CCR's legal director at that time, Bill Goodman answered the question while parenthetically supplying the reason the Center has been in business since a shaky beginning in 1966: "My job is to defend the Constitution from its enemies. Its main enemies right now are the Justice Department and the White House." Considering the prevailing zeitgeist, the statement could not have been more defiant.

The Bush administration announced that its prisoners under the military order would be held at Guantánamo (GITMO). If anyone knew the full significance of this development, it was Ratner. In the early nineties the first

President Bush and then Bill Clinton had used the Guantánamo facility to hold HIV-positive Haitian refugees. Ratner, on behalf of the Center and with the help of a handful of other litigators and activists, forced the government to bring the refugees to the United States. Clearly, the argument would again be made that Guantánamo is a law-free zone, beyond the reach of U.S. courts. And so, at the Center, the search for a client was begun without knowing for certain if, when one was found, a court could also be found that would agree to hear the case. In his book about the Supreme Court, *The Nine*, Jeffrey Toobin says the idea that despised men being held captive at GITMO "might be able to challenge their incarceration in an American courtroom . . . seemed close to outlandish."

In January 2002 the first twenty prisoners were brought to the Naval Station. The Center had its clients: Shafiq Rasul and Asif Iqbal, British citizens, and David Hicks, an Australian. The case, *Rasul v. Bush*, may well have been as unpromising as any the CCR had ever launched. Two courts disposed of it summarily. But then, to everyone's surprise, the Supreme Court agreed to hear it.

Abruptly, in the eyes of the legal world, the Center for Constitutional Rights became a player. Calls came in from lawyers around the country asking how they could reach out to GITMO detainees. Many were from straight-arrow law firms not remotely attuned to the CCR's politics. Ears pricked up in the funding world as well. The Ford Foundation broke the ice with a grant of $200,000 for the Center's Guantánamo work. A contact from the Reconciliation and Civil Rights wing of Atlantic Philanthropies, the foundation initially funded by Charles F. Feeney's Duty Free Shoppers Group, showed up with an interesting question: if given a million dollars, how would the Center spend it? "I had no answer for him," Ratner remembers. "So he said, 'We're going to give you $50,000 to figure out a plan of how you would use a million or more.'" The plan was evidently to Atlantic's satisfaction; it awarded the Center a $2,500,000 grant over a five-year period.

On June 28, 2004, the Supreme Court, in a six to three decision, handed the Bush administration a stunning defeat by ruling in *Rasul v. Bush* that prisoners held at Guantánamo could not be deprived of their *habeas corpus* rights. Apparently anticipating the decision and doubting the strength of its case, the government had already released Rasul and Iqbal and returned them to the United Kingdom. Hicks was held for trial by a military commission.

The CCR's budget went from $1.2 million at the time of September 11, 2001, to $5.5 million after *Rasul*. In the same period, the CCR staff more than doubled. The skill level of that staff is now widely acknowledged. Following up its groundbreaking work on *Rasul*, the CCR ran Guantánamo training sessions for six hundred lawyers from around the country, the majority of them from high-prestige firms.

All the government's records and documents relating to Guantánamo are sequestered in a secure facility in Washington. They may be examined only at the facility and only by persons who have first obtained a top-secret FBI sensitive compartmentalized security clearance. The same security clearance is required for lawyers visiting clients at GITMO. The CCR's Gutierrez was the first *habeas* attorney permitted to visit a client held at Guantánamo. She calls the clearance process "invasive." "I'm very aware I'm subjected to the kind of monitoring the government wants to do. We have to notify the United States whenever we travel outside the country. We have to agree to be polygraphed if they ask us to be polygraphed." Former legal worker Jessica Baen describes the process: "They make you basically tell them everything that you've done in the past ten years, so where you've gone to school, where you've worked, where you've lived, and somebody who's seen you doing all those things. They talk to you about foreign travel, your financial situation. . . ."

Some of the clients the CCR lawyers acquired were initially hostile. They viewed any American as a representative of the United States government. "These people have been tortured, they've been beaten, so it's very difficult to gain trust, and Center lawyers have been able to do that," Ratner says. It's a skill that's been passed along to visiting attorneys.

The Center continues to represent several detainees, but the focus of its Guantánamo work has shifted to finding countries willing to accept men eligible for release. It has taken the lead in tracking and monitoring detainees who have been released. One purpose, says Vincent Warren, is to help other *habeas* lawyers who are looking for places to resettle their clients. "We're also looking at some of the post-release issues." For example, dealing with reuniting families often torn apart. "If your family is in country X and you're released to country Y," Warren explains, "we then try to work to unify families and to monitor the services that the government offers. It's a significant amount of work, but getting people released from Guantánamo is really only the first step."

Bush's military order propelled the Center into going for broke. The result was that it came from being reviled on bad days and on good days ignored to commanding the kind of credibility it takes to be summoned to a meeting at the White House. A graphic illustration of how far it's traveled on the same journey: in 2009, two hundred attorneys crowded a D.C. District Court hearing. All brought actions contesting the government's latest restrictions placed on its Guantánamo protective order, and the hearing was designed to find a procedure to incorporate the many cases. Tasked by the court with taking charge of the argument: the CCR's Kadidal and Gutierrez.

CHAPTER 2

People's Lawyer

"... it began as a tax-exempt place to supply funds so we could all run around the Deep South without going broke." That's the way lawyer William Kunstler told me the Center for Constitutional Rights got its shaky start forty-odd years ago.

Except not so fast. The way Arthur Kinoy remembered it, he, Kunstler, and fellow attorneys Morton Stavis and Benjamin Smith founded the Center for reasons that were immeasurably more high-minded. The year was 1966. Each of them was already a veteran of civil rights work in the South. They had, Kinoy said, "come very much to the conclusion that it was impossible to function as people's lawyers for the movement without being able to work *together*." For Kinoy, it was the collective experience that was the most essential component.

The differences in the way Kinoy and Kunstler recall why the organization was launched reveal more about the deponents than it does about history. No matter what their respective reasons, Kinoy, Kunstler, Stavis, and Smith founded an organization that would make the courts its battlefield and then see to it that this battlefield extended the very reach of the law.

It was in that same year, 1966, that Catholic bishops in the United States issued their pronouncement that the war in Vietnam must not be permitted to escalate "beyond morally acceptable limits." In that year too, President Lyndon B. Johnson was similarly concerned about escalation, but his focus was on interest rates. He capped them, then assured Americans they could have it all, "guns and butter," war and prosperity. What would soon come to be known as the Freedom Movement was turning America's South into a war zone. It would be contested as fiercely, if less bloodily, as any village or rice paddy in Vietnam.

In 1966, Morton Stavis lived in New Jersey. Kunstler and Kinoy were law partners in New York City. Smith, with a law office in New Orleans, was their southern connection. By distinctly different routes, the four had become deeply involved in providing legal assistance, both civil and criminal, to growing efforts by African Americans in the South to put an end to segregation. Being adamant about the right of black people to register to vote was a principal tactic in those efforts. Sometimes this tactic triggered clashes with law enforcement agents, requiring civil rights attorneys to step briskly to the defense of the accused. Stavis once told a film crew that the result of repeatedly crossing paths while they were engaged in those struggles was that "Arthur and I and Bill and Ben Smith became a quartet."

It became primarily the Mississippi Challenge that compelled members of the quartet to continue to "run around the Deep South." The Challenge was the effort mounted by

African-American voters to discredit the legitimacy of the Democratic Party in Mississippi.

The Mississippi Freedom Democratic Party (MFDP) had been founded in 1963 at a Council of Federated Organizations (COFO) state convention. COFO nailed a powerful thesis to the door of Mississippi's established Democratic Party: so long as the state's black people were systematically denied access to the polls, all balloting results in the state were invalid. MFDP stalwarts showed up in strength at the Democrats' 1964 national convention in Atlantic City with the demand that they, and not the "regular" delegates, were the authentic representatives of all Mississippians. MFDP delegate Fannie Lou Hamer captured the attention of the country with her remarkable declaration that "we are sick and tired of being sick and tired." Their demand to be seated was denied.

Kinoy, Kunstler, Stavis, and a young Mississippi lawyer named William Higgs became the Challenge's attorneys. They developed a tactic that became the MFDP's response to their rebuff at Atlantic City. They asked lawyers from all over the country to come to take sworn testimony from African-American Mississippians who had been turned away when they tried to register as voters, even as Lyndon Johnson and Richard Nixon campaigned for southern electoral votes. The depositions would be presented when the new Congress convened as evidence that the elected representatives from Mississippi should not be seated. The National Lawyers Guild (NLG) offered to coordinate the undertaking, and Stavis agreed to serve as chief counsel to the MFDP leadership.

One hundred fifty-three lawyers answered the call. Victor McTeer was a young Mississippi attorney who would later help anchor the Center for Constitutional Rights' presence in the South. He remembered civil rights leader Fannie Lou Hamer, sparkplug and spirit of the MFDP, telling him that the carpetbagging lawyers "did it in a genteel fashion, getting along with some of Mississippi's most heinous racists, and they did it effectively, putting together testimony that was very convincing for Congress." Stavis described it as "a perfect example of integrating activity of lawyers and the local people."

It was during this phase of the Challenge that Kinoy was called to Washington to argue *Dombrowski v. Pfister* before the Supreme Court. Dr. James Dombrowski, one of the few southern whites to enlist in the civil rights struggle, had been instrumental in organizing the Southern Conference Educational Fund (SCEF). What quickly drew SCEF to the attention of the authorities was that its message was primarily addressed to white workers and farmers. As Kinoy explained, "Jim was telling them, 'your future lies with an alliance with the black movements.'" At that time, the notion that class and race distinctions could be discarded—that poor people could join forces without respect to color—was incendiary. The culture of the South since Emancipation had relied on poor whites accepting their impoverished condition because they could at least claim social superiority to blacks.

In October 1963, Dombrowski, Ben Smith, and Smith's law partner Bruce Waltzer were arrested in Louisiana for subversion and failure to register a subversive organization. The "subversive" organizations were identified as the Southern Conference Educational Fund and the National Lawyers Guild. Louisiana's anti-subversive laws were graphic examples of the way local authorities had learned to bend anticommunist preoccupations in Washington to their own purposes: in this instance, the effective elimination of two left organizations and three civil rights activists. In his autobiography, *Rights On Trial*, Kinoy said the Dombrowski case brought into focus the "atmosphere of fear and intimidation [that] would paralyze the Freedom Movement, first in Louisiana and then throughout the South."

Kinoy was attending a National Lawyers Guild workshop in New Orleans when he received news of the arrests of his colleagues. He urged Smith and Waltzer to attack the constitutionality of the laws they were charged with violating: Louisiana's anti-subversive statutes. He wanted the state to be hauled into a federal court and made to explain why people working to make sure that civil rights were available equally to all citizens could be accused of committing a crime.

With Smith threatened with prison and Kinoy arguing before the Supreme Court to keep him out, Kunstler taking on all comers in the Deep South, and Stavis counseling the Mississippi Challenge, it was a heady if frenzied time. During this period, as Stavis remembered it, he and the other three spoke to each other almost every night from wherever they were: "We were a team."

It was out of this intensity and teamwork that an idea took shape. Yes they were a team, but what they needed was a structure, not much but enough to provide a base for raising the money they needed to be able to continue their work. The quartet contacted wealthy New York attorney Robert Boehm, inviting him to come down and take a look at what they were up to. "They had an idea that an organization was needed," Boehm said. "They wanted to involve me." He went.

In *Dombrowski v. Pfister*, argued by Kinoy, the Supreme Court ruled that the Louisiana statutes under which

Dombrowski, Smith, and Waltzer had been convicted were an "overly broad regulation of speech." It was the beginning of what was to become known as the "Dombrowski remedy," the use of a federal injunction against a state criminal prosecution. "Dombrowski suits" quickly became popular tools. When states attacked civil rights and antiwar activists, lawyers would fight back with *Dombrowski.*

In his autobiography, Kinoy interpreted organizing the Center as "a coming of age for us in terms of understanding our own role and responsibilities." He was keenly aware that being a lawyer is, as he styled it, "one of the most egocentric of professions." Certainly none of the four could be accused of reticence when it came to taking either charge or bows. Kinoy believed they had to find a way to make sure their aggressiveness remained in the service of their beliefs rather than of their appetites for self-promotion. "[W]e had come to recognize the need for people's lawyers to find ways of working together in an ongoing planning group, tied to each other by mutual commitment."

Maybe. Bill Kunstler would have been the first to admit that he deserved to be rated among the more egocentric in the most egocentric of professions. When he spoke to me about the Center's beginnings, there wasn't a hint of planning groups or mutual commitments, nor did he mention anything about maturing to a new level of understanding of his responsibilities. He discussed looking for a basis of financial support for the group's civil rights work. He had been relying for that support first on the Gandhi Society for Human Rights and then on Ethel Clyde, a "very wealthy lady." She funneled money to the quartet through the Unitarian Church in New Orleans, which "allowed her contributions to be [tax] deductible."

The group's dependence on the ongoing generosity of a single benefactor was problematic. Kunstler said the time came when he and the others decided they should formalize the work they were doing in the South "with an organization that we had more control over." He fully expected the new organization would have a life span limited to the work its founders were doing in the South. "I thought of it as an ad hoc organization to furnish legal help to the civil rights movement. The idea was it wouldn't be a membership organization like the ACLU and it wouldn't be dominated by one organization like the NAACP Legal Defense Fund. It would be more catholic."

Stavis's son George suggests yet another impetus for the Center's founding. He maintains it was his father's conviction that the Center grew quite logically out of that feature of the Mississippi Challenge that brought lawyers from around the country to Mississippi for the purpose of taking testimony from people deprived of their voting rights. At the time, Morton Stavis saw a need for a place to which all these lawyers from the Challenge could turn for advice and counsel if they wanted to keep working on civil rights projects. "So if there's a lawyer out in Kalamazoo of progressive mind but who is terrorized by his local legal establishment," George recalls his father telling him, "we'll give him help and succor. We'll give him expertise. We'll show him how to use the federal courts. We'll be the backup, the research department. We'll provide resources—mental, not financial—to progressive people around the country. And we'll keep this interconnection that may have come into focus at the Mississippi Challenge." Those widely scattered attorneys provided a cohort for the four lawyers and, in turn, the efforts being made by the same far-flung attorneys on behalf of the civil rights movement were strengthened by the fledgling organization, which provided necessary backup and encouragement.

Mort Stavis held that he, Kinoy, Kunstler, and Smith were each very different personalities and very independent people. What made them such a successful team, he believed, were their shared goals and objectives. "The fact that we had those common objectives overcame individual differences and helped develop and project the team and ultimately the CCR."

As one of the few National Lawyers Guild members in Louisiana at the time, Ben Smith could hardly fail to encounter the civil rights attorneys who were starting to make their way down from the North. "Bruce [Waltzer, Smith's law partner] and Ben were the only white lawyers in Louisiana then who were willing and anxious to work together with us in defense of the black movement and in defense of the whole right-to-vote movement," Kinoy recalled. Of Smith's role in starting the Center, Kunstler said, "to have a white southerner and non-Jew was very important. At the beginning we had nothing in the North. It was all in the South. So Ben was important."

It was important, too, that Smith's law firm was located in New Orleans. Not only is the federal judiciary's Fifth Circuit, the circuit dealing with the Deep South, based in New Orleans but Smith's office provided the team with what Kunstler called "a place to roost."

With Kinoy offering an abundance of vision and Stavis the nuts-and-bolts organizational skills, incorporation papers for the Civil Rights Legal Defense Fund were filed in Newark on September 9, 1966. The name was changed to Law Center for Constitutional Rights in February of the next year. "Law" was dropped from the name in March

1970. Kinoy, from his strategic position on the faculty of Rutgers University School of Law, persuaded the dean to let the new organization set up its office on the school's campus. That provident arrangement lasted only a few months. "The dean was friendly," Robert Boehm recalled, "but he got into trouble with his faculty who were much more conservative." So the organization, with Dennis Roberts as its sole staff attorney, and one secretary, Lillian Green, removed itself to the fifth floor of the RKO Theater Building at 116 Market Street in downtown Newark.

The burden of rent and salaries was when Robert Boehm's reconnaissance visit to the South paid off: he contributed $40,000 to cover the inaugural year's expenses. Margaret Thompson, Stavis's secretary, dropped in from time to time to keep the books. Stavis guided the process of incorporating as a non-profit organization in New Jersey. "Arthur and I knew from nothing about forming corporations," Kunstler said. "Luckily we had Morty who knew all that and could do all the leg work . . . with Internal Revenue to make it tax deductible." Without benefit of title, Stavis became the Center's first executive director. Kunstler had no doubt about how vital Stavis's contribution was in those early months: "Without him there would be no Center, no question about it." Smith was named president.

By the end of the first year, the founders had installed a Board of Officers and Trustees composed of themselves plus two outside attorneys and an eighteen-member Board of Legal Advisors. In addition, the complement of staff attorneys had been raised to three. Records from the time don't break down individual salaries, but given that the entire staff was paid $19,843, plainly no one was getting rich. The year closed with the books balanced and a surplus of $2,783.

The Law Center's first annual report was issued in 1967. It was titled *Docket Report* and contained a mere fifteen pages. It wasted no time trumpeting the arrival of yet another hard-charging task force in the service of truth, virtue, justice, and the rest. Instead, in two succinct paragraphs, the report stated why the founders believed themselves compelled to enter the already clamorous competition for civil rights litigation dollars:

> The Law Center was formed because the individual attorneys who joined together to become its trustees were concerned over the absence of affirmative legal techniques in the area of civil liberties and civil rights, to supplement the traditional defense work in this field. They recognized, of course, the extraordinary value of the organizations for legal defense which have been operating effectively in this field for many years. But it seemed to them that there was a need for *creative experimentation in the development of new legal approaches* [emphasis added] whose major thesis would be that litigation, besides its obvious defensive purpose, could also, and perhaps primarily, become an affirmative means of preserving individual liberties and freedom.

The operative words in their *Docket Report* are "affirmative" and "creative."

Any attempt to understand what's unique about Center cases, why they're taken and how they're litigated, has to include an understanding of the significance of those two words when applied to the law. In its work in the South, the Law Center was both creative and affirmative in adopting the new "Dombroski remedy." One example is the defense of the Student Nonviolent Coordinating Committee (SNCC).

SNCC was among the more aggressive of the black liberation groups. As such, its workers were favorite targets of state legal actions. Charges were brought in Alabama (*Carmichael v. Selma* and *Wright v. Montgomery*), in Georgia (*Carmichael v. Allen*), in Tennessee (*Brooks v. Briley*), and in Ohio (*Burks v. Schott*). In each case, the Law Center fought back with *Dombrowski.* It did the same on behalf of civil rights organizers in Massachusetts (*Landrum v. Richardson*) and in Kentucky (*Baker v. Bindner*). This all took place in the first year of the organization's existence.

Georgetown University professor and CCR board member David Cole says the philosophy of litigation at the Center is to "make an affirmative case" even when the case is essentially defensive, that is, when it involves a client accused of a crime. One way to do that, he explains, is to use a case as a teaching and organizing tool. The case then "becomes a focal point of a debate. It's a dramatic forum in which to raise issues."

Board member Ellen Yaroshefsky suggests affirmation and innovation can be functions of political perspective. The Center, in her view, sees a given case not simply for its legal issues but for the impact those issues might have on a community, a gender, or a population. "Nobody is willing to take on the margins, and that's what the CCR has always done. While other groups will talk about rights, women's rights, we're somehow able, as a result of a political perspective, to put together the rights of women, the rights of poor people, the rights of people of color, the rights of children and figure out how to bring a case to combine all of those issues and then spearhead people looking at it that way."

"The Center has never been afraid to leap ahead in new fields and be at the cutting edge," said onetime Wall Street attorney and Center volunteer Mahlon Perkins. "Whatever the new problems are that come along, they've been in the forefront." The role of the Center is equivalent to what the military might call a strike force or first line of defense. They recognize in emerging issues—women's health, international human rights—the potential for organizing around legal challenges. They offer their services at what one CCR lawyer called "the cutting moment."

If a case seems to hold a potential for breaking new ground, the CCR's interest in it quickens. If the case revisits ground already fought for, and if other law groups have already joined the fray, the Center will usually refer the applicant to other attorneys. It thinks of itself, said the late board member and onetime staff attorney Rhonda Copelon, "as less institutionalizing an issue than . . . creating the principles and moving from there."

Former staff attorney Matthew Chachere pointed out a problem inherent in the CCR's emphasis on innovation: law is an intrinsically conservative institution. "So when you go in front of a judge—and they tend to be white, middle-class males—you tend to say that all the opinions that have gone before are consistent with what you're trying to say, because if a judge says, 'that's a new, creative, novel idea,' you know you're in trouble."

In trouble or not, the Center from the beginning made new, creative, novel ideas its meat and potatoes, the specialty of the house. Served up with an impact case, untested ideas creatively applied are the pride of the Center menu.

Impact cases come in two varieties: those that leave an imprint on the law and others that advance the unique goals of a community. *Dombrowski* was an impact case. *Rasul*, as we saw in the preceding chapter, was another. Cases with potential impact are hard to come by and even harder to win. But "winning" is defined differently at the Center than in most law offices.

While the likelihood of prevailing in court has always been weighed at the CCR, it has seldom by itself determined whether a case is accepted or rejected. If the case is brought, what lessons will be learned from it? Will it function as an organizing catalyst? In Center terms, it's possible to claim victory even when the legal action fails. Minds both in and out of the legal profession may have been changed. An inchoate movement may have sharpened its focus in the process of helping attorneys prepare for court. The court battles may have bucked up a movement's dispirited leaders. Almost always, the case spreads news of the movement's existence and so helps it attract adherents.

Guantánamo is a vivid example of the way the Center keeps score. CCR development director Kevi Brannelly points out that you can *appear* to win Supreme Court cases and lose the battle:

> People are still there. It's really hard to say, "We did this and the gates were opened and everybody went home." On the other hand, because of the litigation we were able to find out who was down there and how they were being treated and the abuses and to connect them to their families and to do media work so that it stayed in the public eye, and so all of these other groups had information, from small community groups, small churches, synagogues concerned about torture to much larger organizations that had been a little leery about going in early on. . . . But if you can get information out there, if you can push people, it was huge in that case. If nobody had done that, there would still be 800 people down

there instead of 200. And who knows how they'd be treated? The measurement is sometimes difficult for people.

The Center's first annual report lays out a second doctrine, a corollary to the injunction to be creative and affirmative: "[T]he judicial system can become a vital part of a *positive program to protect* [emphasis added] the functioning of our democratic system." More than anything, it was the Supreme Court's ruling in *Dombrowski* that led the founders to that galvanizing conclusion. Henceforth, they were convinced, the federal judiciary, if skillfully and creatively utilized, could be a powerful weapon against courts, legislatures, and law enforcement officials engaged in depriving people of their constitutional liberties. Indeed, the founders' faith in the law as a positive force went even further. Not only, they believed, was the law, when innovatively employed, available to redress specific grievances, it was available to do nothing less than to effect social change.

Jules Lobel, professor of law at the University of Pittsburgh and CCR's vice president, calls cases with the potential to bring about social change "prophetic litigation." He cites lawsuits brought by abolitionists and suffragists as historical examples of how even unsuccessful cases may focus and catalyze movements for social change.

Margaret and Alan McSurely were charged in 1967 with violating Kentucky's sedition laws. Stavis took up their defense in 1970 and persuaded his colleagues to let him run the case through the Center. This development at once altered the office's mission. Civil rights could no longer be said to be its sole concern. The group had no way to know that with the McSurely case they were stepping into an arena that would come to command more of their attention than any other, namely government misconduct. For example, regarding the war in Vietnam, the founders noted in their first annual report that "[T]he very recent pronouncement by General Hershey [head of the draft board] to the effect that students involved in protest demonstrations may for that reason be considered delinquent and have their draft status affected, poses obvious constitutional questions . . ."

In 1969, the Law Center left New Jersey and set up offices at 588 Ninth Avenue in New York City. Its budget had tripled and its staff had grown to five lawyers and three secretaries (who by this time, in a prefiguring of political correctness, were being called 'legal workers').

The trick to hiring lawyers was to find people willing to pass up a high-paying salary in favor of a chance to help people deprived of justice by a harsh social order. The war in Vietnam was giving a sizable portion of a generation an excuse to rebel against what they saw as the oppressive bourgeois values of their parents. It divided the country and brought about a highly charged political atmosphere. In this climate, it was easy for the Center to recruit recent law school graduates who were fired with ideals compatible with the Center's mission. Many who attended law school in the late 1960s had been rudely awakened by the time they emerged into the social ferment three years later. They were looking for ways to save the world using the shiny new tool they'd just acquired.

Not easy. The law is a game designed to make sure any change in how it's played comes glacially and incrementally. Poverty law was beginning to show signs of life in storefront offices but the place sending out the most intriguing vibes was this small office on the East Coast called the Law Center for Constitutional Rights.

Within the first three years of its founding, the organization the quartet began in order to keep their team running around the South had become a significant warrior in the battles devoted to righting social wrongs where the weapon of choice is the law. The next years, however, plunged them into a different struggle, this one with the bailiff.

CHAPTER 3

We Were Just Winging It

Despite its new place of business, much of the Center's work continued to be done in Newark (and its New Jersey incorporation continues). Furthermore, it's where you went, to the Broad Street offices of Stavis, Rossmore, Richardson & Koenigsberg if you were a staff attorney and wanted to consult with Stavis. The privilege of consulting with Stavis, of course, was probably why you accepted the Center's offer of a heavy workload for short money in the first place.

The year 1969 also saw the advent of Peter Weiss as a voluntary staff attorney. As distinct from full-time paid staff attorneys, voluntary staff attorneys work closely with the staff, may be available for assignment, and sometimes keep office space at the Center. Not infrequently, lawyers continue their connection to the CCR by becoming volunteers after they resign their staff positions. The ranks of volunteers include attorneys to whom the Center offers an opportunity to do movement work after they retire from active practice.

A New York lawyer with a specialty in trademark law and an abiding interest in international law, Weiss's exposure to the CCR as a volunteer quickly made him realize he didn't want to go on practicing trademark law full-time. He told his partners he'd henceforth be cutting his contribution to the office approximately in half. At the Center, he was given a desk and a key to the front door. He promptly became, along with Stavis, Kinoy, and Kunstler, one of the "seniors," what Stavis called the "geriatric team" and others on the staff called the "alte kahkas." Weiss has been a member of the Center's board of directors ever since.

Inevitably and with gathering momentum, the CCR was drawn into the legal entanglements growing out of the clamorous actions around the country protesting the war in Vietnam. Most demonstrators came and went peaceably, but invariably some clashed with police and wound up in jail. Overworked movement lawyers responded to the Center's standing offer of moral and professional support. Anti-war litigation thus came to dominate the Center's docket in the first half of the seventies. Given staff members' close identification with the peace movement, it was a heady time.

As the chaotic 1960s came to an end, Kunstler's fame soared with his role in the defense of the "Chicago 7"—Dave Dellinger, Rennie Davis, Abbie Hoffman, John Froines, Tom Hayden, Jerry Rubin, and Lee Weiner (reduced from eight when Bobby Seale was severed from the case). The charge against the accused was violation of a federal anti-riot law growing out of disruptions outside the Democratic Party's national convention in Chicago in 1968. To go with his newly acquired notoriety, Kunstler's comportment in the stormy six-month-long trial earned him twenty-four citations for contempt of court and a jail sentence of four years and thirteen days. Stavis got all but two of the citations dismissed on appeal, and Kunstler served no jail time. The sometimes exasperating fallout for the Center was that their organization became widely known thereafter as "Bill Kunstler's CCR."

Meanwhile, the CCR, consistent with its reliance on creativity, developed its own strategy for coming to the aid of the antiwar movement. The government had developed a tactic of using grand jury subpoenas for incitement or conspiracy to neutralize peace activists. The CCR chose these grand jury cases as its battleground.

"The government brought these actions very fast," says ex-staff attorney James Reif. "They'd issue a subpoena totally out of the blue on Monday ordering you to appear in front of a grand jury on Wednesday." Often a witness who refused to testify was scheduled for contempt hearings the very next day. Center lawyers, pressed by the government's accelerating attack, were, Reif says, "going berserk." They made up the legal arguments as they went along. Their inexperience helped; they were too young and too brash to be slowed down by anything as inconsequential as ignorance.

Nancy Stearns, a contemporary of Reif's, recalls that period as "an era when youth was everything. We were thrown headlong into something that was so much above what our abilities were, but that was okay, we were going to do it." She says when she thinks back to some of the briefs she wrote it's with the startling realization that she was making up theories and wasn't even aware of it. "But that's what Morty and Bill and Arthur had done in the South. They had just made it up. So that we were making it up seemed perfectly logical to them. We didn't have somebody saying to us, 'No, you can't do this because that's not what the law is, there's nothing there to go on.' They would say, 'All right, go and do it.' As a result, we had a confidence that I think was beyond our capabilities."

"I was an associate in a Wall Street law firm," remembers Mark Amsterdam, "one of the ten largest law firms in the country." It was September 1970, and Amsterdam was still in his first year of practicing law. "Someone came into my office and said there was a group called the Center for Constitutional Rights, about which I'd never heard, that wanted a lawyer to go to Okinawa to do military law, about which I knew nothing." Amsterdam pauses in his account as he hunts for a way to make sense of the quixotic thing he'd done so many years earlier. "I was doing corporate debentures and convertible securities." Then he looks at me, spreads his hands in concession, and says, "It was the middle of the Vietnam War . . . I'd never tried a case." He was clearly baffled by the memory, unbelieving. "Mort says, 'the only way to do it is to do it, to go in and you'll do it and you'll be fine.'"

The injunction is vintage Center operating procedure: if you're young and alone against a battery of powerful and experienced attorneys, you'll work harder, dig deeper, and be more creative. You'll seldom doubt that your sense of mission, when combined with a sort of vision quest, a zeal for discovery, not of the self but of the outer limits of what jurisprudence is customarily about, goes a long way toward overcoming the absurd odds you're prepared to face in courtrooms. Most important, you'll be driven not by the promise of a partnership in the firm with its attendant bounty but by a belief that a compatriot, a comrade in the movement, has sent out a distress signal and you're charging to the rescue.

"The movement." It's not a term that lends itself to precise definition. Anyone professing an allegiance to left politics is familiar with it. It's the aggregate of all activists organizing their communities and constituencies, large or small, to bring about a more just society. It's the ongoing struggle by those same organizers to take some of the pain out of the hardships of an unfair social order. Within the movement are movements, popular campaigns waged against specific foes.

Amsterdam explains how the Center for Constitutional Rights, from its headquarters in New York City, came to the decision to open a branch office in such an improbable place as Okinawa. His tale reveals how seriously Center people take the obligation they've accepted to respond when the movement calls, and to be its legal arm. "There was an antiwar activist on Okinawa who had been writing letters to the Center saying, 'We could use a lawyer here, and we could organize around the antiwar sentiment here among the G.I.s.' That was the project. I was going to go over and represent antiwar G.I.s in administrative proceedings and courts martial." Almost all of the troops on their way to and from Vietnam went through Okinawa.

Amsterdam remembers that just before he left, somebody thought to ask if he could get along with black G.I.s, and he wondered how he could have been expected to know. He'd led a relatively cloistered life in school and on Wall Street. Where was he supposed to have interacted with people even moderately unlike his peers, let alone with black men and women in the armed services?

The very possibly doomed nature of the whole enterprise, Amsterdam concedes, was arguably given the cover of legitimacy by how cheap he came. "They bought two round-trip tickets, one for me and one for my girlfriend, and agreed to pay us a living stipend, which turned out to be about $150 a month."

Amsterdam agreed to go for six months and stayed for two years. Among his many cases, he represented a psychological operations staff sergeant who refused to write out a program for a nuclear attack on Korea on the grounds that it was against the Geneva Convention and therefore an unlawful order; Navy people who did conscientious discharge applications; and there were also a number of hardship discharges. "Whatever we could do to get guys out, we did . . . I did thirty-five or forty trials. Thousands of G.I.s came to us." In his spare time he organized an alternative newspaper and helped start a coffeehouse patterned after ones back home that offered havens to antiwar G.I.s.

It can't, of course, be called a typical CCR operation. Not even they send lawyers every day 7,500 miles to hector a war. Still, it had the Center's distinctive M.O. It was more affirmative than defensive. It helped educate. It helped organize. It provided legal services to people who didn't know where else to turn. And it attracted enemies.

The House Committee on Un-American Activities issued a lengthy report charging that the CCR had unlimited financing for its Okinawa project, that it had received grants to continue the project, some for as much as $100,000.

"One of my clients," Amsterdam recalls, "found a classified document describing the project, accusing us of being subversive, and saying we were getting funding from drug money. I don't think I ever got more than $250 in a month, and that wasn't only for us to live on but it was to run a law office." Amsterdam savored the memory of his own private battle of Okinawa: "That was my entry into the movement."

When Amsterdam returned to New York, he didn't go back to Wall Street; instead, he put in another three years at the Center as a staff attorney. "I always felt that the Center enabled me to do some work in a short period of time where if I never did anything of consequence again in my life I could at least say, 'I did something that at the time was important, that helped a lot of people.' I can look back at that time and say, 'Yes, I was where I was supposed to be.' I loved it."

Like Amsterdam, Janice Goodman has to laugh at how little prepared she was in the early 1970s for what she was asked to do and at how little that mattered. "We had a lot of guts because we didn't have much legal experience." She recalls how young attorneys received little guidance. "It wasn't like you go to Wall Street and for ten years you have someone who mentors you until you know what you're doing."

She tells of the time she represented a doctor who was being criminally prosecuted in New Jersey for performing an abortion, and something serious happened to the woman. The doctor came to the CCR because by then it was well known for its work on abortion law. Goodman had only recently been admitted to the bar. She moved in federal court to get a temporary restraining order on behalf of the doctor. "We lost. I call Nancy [Stearns] . . . 'What do you think we should do next?' She says you'll have to appeal to the Court of Appeals. I say, 'What do you mean?' The next thing I know I'm on a train going down to the Court of Appeals in Philadelphia. There I am with my little motion asking for an expedited hearing for a stay. Of course I'm denied and I say, 'Okay, I can go home.' I call Nancy and tell her what happened and she says, 'Well, we'll just have to go to the Supreme Court.' The next day, on the way down to Washington, I wrote papers on a yellow pad on why we should get this temporary restraining order. We lost, but it's an example of how you got thrown into things. That was a tremendous learning experience. We were very young, very enthusiastic." Whether the doctor who paid the price of Goodman's inexperience shared her enthusiasm is open to question.

Dorothy M. Zellner, a veteran of the Freedom Movement in the South, holds the record for length of tenure at the CCR. She served in a variety of capacities, including office manager and supervisor of the intern program. A continuing problem she had with her work with the Center was the low rate of pay for staff people. When asked why she stayed on so long, she answers, "When you have a few moments of knowing that what you're doing is meaningful, it goes a long way."

An occasional criticism of the Center had been that the founders hit on a scheme to provide themselves with an abundance of first-rate assistance at rock-bottom prices. These critics further believed that the CCR, like so many left groups, relied on those meaningful "few moments" to provide the rewards for working long hours for very little money.

When Ron Daniels became executive director in 1994, he struggled to push past an entrenched system of equal pay for everyone, attorneys and legal workers alike, without consideration given to length of time on the job. He insisted CCR lawyers should be paid at least on the same scale as Legal Aid and Legal Services lawyers. "If we were to bring in the best lawyers, how do you pay them all the same? If somebody says, '[W]ell, I'm willing to come, but this is what I need,' how do you do that in relation to somebody else? These were questions that became killers. We worked them out reasonably well." To this day, people who work at the CCR have to be motivated more by the opportunity to do work they believe in than by the money they're able to make. But the rates of pay aren't as Dickensian as they were at one time.

In 1969, *The New York Times* asked Sidney E. Zion to direct his gimlet eye on the Center for Constitutional Rights. What Zion discovered astonished him: "Imagine," he wrote, "a law firm where the staff is on salary but the partners work for nothing? And the clients pay no fees? And nobody's afraid to lose cases?"

The fundamental mission of the Center at this time was driven by the conviction that anywhere people were fighting for social justice, that's where the Center had to be. The rapid growth of grand jury and contempt cases in this period was forcing it, as we've seen, to expand its docket beyond civil rights. The outlines of a paradox are at once discernible. In its civil rights litigation, the CCR pioneered ways to make the federal government its partner in its attacks on white supremacy laws. That strategy remained in place in the Deep South; the CCR continued to enlist the federal judiciary under the banner of the civil rights movement. The grand jury cases cast that very same judiciary as an arm of the antiwar movement's most relentless enemies.

As the decade of the seventies began, Attorney General John Mitchell's Department of Justice was bent on stifling the growing demand for peace in Southeast Asia. His strategy was to criminalize activists by ordering them to appear before grand juries and so render the peace movement leaderless. The federal judiciary, with few exceptions, played the role assigned to it. Judges acted as agents of the U.S. Attorney's office, frequently threatening witnesses with jail if they didn't answer the government's questions.

This made it necessary for the Center to fall back on more traditional tactics, which it acknowledges in its third annual report: "While affirmative litigation in the federal courts remains a useful tool in some cases, the protection of constitutional rights in the courts has more recently put civil rights and constitutional lawyers in the position of developing sophisticated defensive techniques as well. Thus the criminal process and the development of tools for the effective defensive representation of persons striving for social change has recently occupied much of the attention of the Center."

Spurred by the urgency of the demand for their services, Center attorneys charged hell-bent into the grand jury cases. Rapid response was the name of the game, hubris the attitude of choice.

James Reif, a lawyer with a private practice in lower Manhattan, remembers his work as a Center staff attorney involving a high-energy level along with a sense of purpose. "What sticks in my mind now so many years later was the pace," says Reif. "We were doing an incredible number of cases, each of which required an incredible amount of work, each of which was very important, and we were doing it all with limited resources. We were flying all over the goddamn place . . . and we were also training lawyers as we were going along. All these [grand jury] decisions are real short, they come out real quickly, they're not reported, so we're sending this stuff to people all over the country, trying to give them stuff to use in their cases."

Anywhere the Justice Department's internal security division lawyers would show up, the CCR's team would show up. It was as if the Center team thought of themselves as the Harlem Globetrotters playing the Washington Generals. "We would play them before a different judge in city after city."

Because of the absence of precedent, there was no one to give guidance. "We were just winging it," Reif says. "We'd pick everybody's brains." Center lawyers, joined by colleagues from the National Lawyers Guild, codified their experience in the form of a manual on representing witnesses before grand juries. It remains today the standard text.

At the same time civil rights and government misconduct were vying for energy and resources at the Center, yet another major category of litigation was beginning to take shape and demand recognition. The new issue was women's rights. At the outset, it was women's health as affected by the abortion question. This was the end of the 1960s, the early days of the women's movement, and the issue wasn't embraced by everyone at the Center. All the same, mostly because it gave the group a chance to get back on the offensive, women's rights soon came to be anointed a movement even by the skeptics at the Center.

Nancy Stearns headed the CCR team put together to challenge abortion laws. She said that when she became a staff attorney in 1969 the potential for legal action around attempts being made to wrest control of women's bodies away from male-dominated legislatures was barely discernible. "It wasn't," Stearns says, "something anyone really had any consciousness of."

Unfortunately, at the time, that same ignorance often informed the way women were treated in the office, particularly by the Center's founders. Stearns remains convinced gender was a source of less friction at the Center than it was in most offices during that period, possibly owing to the group's small size. "When I first got hired, there was the staff—some men and some women—and there was Morty, Arthur, and Bill. The women's question didn't exist at CCR."

Former staff attorney Elizabeth M. Schneider is equally prepared to grant the Center's elders a degree of absolution: "Given who these guys were and that the women's movement was a revolution that was happening, I think they did well. They tried very hard to hear what people were saying to them. They didn't always understand, and sometimes it took a long time. It was sometimes easier for them to deal with these issues in the context of cases than it was in terms of the process and structure of the Center itself." While acknowledging that gender issues did occasionally intrude themselves, Schneider nonetheless insists that the CCR ". . . wasn't an institution like so many at that time that came to the edge of destruction as a result of generational or gender problems."

CCR attorneys responded quickly to women who were beginning to come to the realization that the burden of restrictive abortion laws might be lifted more readily by courts than by legislatures. Their quickness off the mark isn't surprising. CCR's female staff attorneys were aware of tactical decisions as soon as they were made by movement leaders; indeed, they were often themselves part of that very decision-making process. "We were all activists," says one-time staff attorney Janice Goodman. "We were in the field."

When developments occurred in the movement, Stearns was often forced to press for a CCR response. That meant getting the attention of the seniors, not easy given their obliviousness. "[C]ertainly at the CCR women's issues were not taken seriously, not even close," Stearns said. Rhonda Copelon recalled that the elders simply didn't see the abortion issue as being on the cutting edge of a new movement. "Morty used to say, 'I'm totally for a woman's right to abortion.' But . . . [h]e didn't understand it as political the way he understood racism as political."

Nonetheless, Stearns kept up the pressure, believing Stavis especially could be educated. In due course, Stavis brought Kunstler and Kinoy into the fold, and the CCR joined the drive to invalidate New York's criminal abortion law in 1970. When Copelon joined the Center a year later, women's rights litigation already commanded a significant position on the Center's docket. She said it was only over time that she came to understand how much opposition Stearns had to overcome to make that transition possible.

The Center's work on women's health cases put pressure on organizations like the ACLU to view the right to an abortion from the woman's perspective rather than from the doctor's. Copelon cited the Center's innovative approach in women's health cases as "an example of being willing to take on and move other institutions into much more controversial stances." By changing the angle of attack from the traditional one of a doctor's right to decide what's best for his patient to a woman's right to decide what's best for herself, the CCR succeeded in raising a whole range of women's rights: to privacy, equal protection, and freedom from religious doctrine.

The timing was fortuitous. As the civil rights movement began its decline, so too had the CCR's fortunes, despite its overflowing antiwar docket. Women's rights gave the organization a new basis for recognition and a new group of supporters. Former legal director Frank Deale remembers women's rights being "a tremendous moneymaker for the Center." Janice Goodman says the abortion cases drew wide attention and gave the CCR "more up-front recognition than anything else at the time." Cases were brought not only in New York and New Jersey but also in Rhode Island and Massachusetts. The organization was extending its reach. A longer reach meant wider name recognition which in turn translated into a broader donor base. Adding to this potential for fundraising were coordinating relationships developed with lawyers in other states, as well as with more traditional organizations such as the National Organization of Women and Planned Parenthood.

It wasn't merely the potential for fundraising, however, that ultimately won the full dedication of the seniors to the cause of women's rights. It was when they saw the possibilities for organizing that they became fully committed to the women's movement. Organizing, most notably for Kinoy, was what set the CCR apart.

When Nancy Stearns says her work on abortion cases was "probably as exciting as anything I have ever done and will ever do," she is talking about more than court battles. Just as the seniors had learned from her, they in turn taught her that a lawsuit could be not only a hammer with which to beat a defendant into submission but also an anvil on which to shape an entire movement.

For a young and impassioned attorney, it was a revelation. That was the good news. The bad news was the toll the work often took. Close identification with client and cause made keeping an arm's-length relationship all but impossible. Every lawyer, of course, wants to win. Winning is ennobling. This is especially true when the case arouses the lawyer's passion, a relatively commonplace occurrence in movement law. At the same time, it's hard to appreciate the accomplishments when the process has left the lawyer overwhelmed by a sense of outrage. The CCR's abortion cases often triggered profoundly negative emotions, even in victory. Stearns recalls: "I got burned out doing abortion cases at some point, because I was so angry. I got to a point where I could not be in a courtroom with those lawyers for the anti-abortion people."

If victory could leave attorneys feeling bitter and unfulfilled, defeat could be calamitous. Everyone working at the Center understands that cases are often taken when chances of success in the conventional sense are remote. With the abortion cases in particular, expectations ran high. This was a cause whose time had so clearly come that the idea of failure was unacceptable. Still, there were times when no matter how total the commitment or creative and ardent the litigator, the Center was unable to prevail, and the lawyers had to accept that they couldn't help people to whom they'd formed remarkably close attachments. Stearns calls such times "horrendous."

The symbiosis at the CCR of law and organizing developed out of the politics of the founders. They were men for whom political conviction was the central organizing principle of their lives. Pursuing legal goals without having first analyzed the place those goals occupied in a broader social and political context was foreign to their natures. Certainly Kinoy's vision of the Center from the beginning, as he wrote in his autobiography some years later, included the placing of its lawyers' legal skills at the service of people trying to organize themselves to bring about social change. In his autobiography, he defined "the driving motivation of a people's lawyer" to be helping popular movements organize and function.

The late Haywood Burns, once Center vice president, confirmed this, saying that the connection between legal work and organizational work was present from the beginning. There was, he said, "always a tie to the local communities and to movements." However, according to Burns, it wasn't until the founders had a chance to lift their heads and look at what they'd created that they could spell out the doctrine of a movement-driven law office. The connection became more conscious, more purposeful, and more explicit as time passed. "It became more a part of the stated agenda. But it was always there."

By 1976, the era of Chief Justice Earl Warren's liberal Supreme Court was over. The Court in that year approved the death penalty and limited the ability of federal courts to order new trials when state courts played fast and loose with the Constitution. In the same year, the Court restricted the Fourth Amendment's guarantee against unreasonable searches. Moreover, Nixon and Ford appointees were beginning to dominate the federal bench. Groundbreaking law cases such as *Brown v. Board of Education*, which led to school desegregation, and to a lesser degree the CCR's *Dombrowski v. Pfister*, were becoming much harder to win.

The Center's Seventh Annual Report, published in 1976, revealed for the first time a tone not only embattled but embittered. It highlighted the CCR's "historic role" to be "a legal instrument of the people; people who are challenging the inequities and injustices of our society. . . ." It went on to describe the Center as being engaged in a struggle for justice and against "illusory" democracy. "We recognize that this struggle arises in countless ways, from criminal defense to labor litigation to affirmative suits for women's rights. But no matter what the issue may be, when the law is used as a weapon and the courtroom as a battlefield, the CCR is committed to insuring that the people never enter the fray unarmed."

The year 1976 marked the organization's tenth anniversary and the commencement of a more formal structure. When Marilyn Boydstun Clement was brought in as executive director, she encountered an infrastructure characterized by non-management. The reluctance of the seniors to step into active leadership roles had resulted in decisions at the Center being madc collectively by consent. And everyone, regardless of their degree of responsibility or the number of years they'd been in place, was paid the same.

Clement broke this pattern by conditioning her acceptance of the job on a higher salary. What's more, she demanded a reorganization of the board of directors. Stavis, who had been overseeing business affairs on an ad hoc basis, was named president. Robert Boehm became chairman. The more conventional structure notwithstanding, few of the Center's board members had the time or the inclination to involve themselves in day-to-day operations. Clement did not have legal training, which meant that, by default, decisionmaking remained in the hands of the collective. Strained board–staff relations would characterize management of the CCR until they attained critical mass in 1994.

As the 1980s began, Michael Ratner, a staff attorney, was named as the CCR's legal director. Creation of this post was another gesture toward structural rationalization for the Center. In this period, its focus shifted to the Caribbean and Central America. In a series of cases, the CCR found ways, some creative indeed, to support dissident movements against repressive governments in El Salvador and Nicaragua, Grenadans opposed to U.S. intervention, Fidelistas, and pro-independence Puerto Ricans. The Center also took up the struggle of a largely church-inspired movement organized to provide sanctuary for refugees from Central American war zones.

Given the unorthodoxy of many of these cases, it's not surprising the CCR caught the attention of a group of women from Berkshire, England, who were demanding that the United States Air Force remove the nuclear-armed Cruise missiles that were being housed at the local Greenham Common Royal Air Force base. They dispatched a delegation to the United States to investigate the possibility of bringing a legal action against the U.S. government, and found their way to the Center, where the case was assessed for its organizing potential. It was also seen as an opportunity to test whether the law could be enlisted against the government on behalf of the antinuclear movement. A federal district court ultimately dismissed the suit on the grounds that its issue was political rather than legal.

However, while *Greenham Women Against Cruise Missiles v. Reagan* was being pressed, women traveled the country, holding public talks about the issues. Out of these meetings and from the arguments presented in court hearings, a crucial bond emerged between the women's and antinuclear movements. Publicity about the case drew wide attention throughout the United States and in Europe. The Center's 1986 Docket Report chronicles the defeat and closes with the assurance that "the CCR is committed to making the law a useful tool in the international struggle against nuclear destruction." Indeed, *Greenham Common*, the Central American, and the sanctuary cases may be said to represent the Center functioning in a manner closest to its founding mission. They were uphill court battles, but they opened wide battlefields on which to engage forces of reaction, all the while seizing opportunities to organize and educate.

The 1980s saw the adoption of three programs designed to extend the Center's outreach. Structure was introduced in 1984 with the inauguration of a Movement Support Network (MSN). The circumstance that more than any other prompted the MSN's formation was a survey the Center conducted that revealed systematic government harassment of groups supporting progressive movements in Nicaragua and El Salvador. The CCR compiled a list of people who were questioned by the FBI after visits to Nicaragua. A California congressman used the list to publicly embarrass FBI director William Webster, and the harassment was curtailed. Further, two Center pamphlets were quickly prepared and distributed by the MSN: *If An Agent Knocks: Federal Investigators and Your Rights,* authored principally by Margaret Ratner Kunstler, and *Radical Re-Entry: Coming Through Customs.*

The MSN provided a base for activists to share news of their actions and to collect useful information. A legal worker was tasked with fielding calls, compiling information, and helping organizers find out what they needed to know. A staff lawyer was assigned to lend assistance. Intelligence gathered by the Network was given exposure in a newsletter and in media releases. In its first year alone, the Network offered aid and comfort to antinuclear, sanctuary, and civil rights groups. Perhaps the MSN's finest hour was when its information exchange uncovered a pattern of harassment against chapters around the country of the Committee in Support of the People of El Salvador (CISPES). This discovery led to a lawsuit; then the Network went on to use the publicity generated by the suit to draw wide attention to the government's political espionage.

A second fundamental development in the 1980s was the Ella Baker Student Program. (Baker was a celebrated civil rights leader in the South.) The program, still strong, allows the Center to benefit from the labor of volunteer interns while giving law students on-the-job training in movement law. Dorothy Zellner was the program's first coordinator. During her tenure, which lasted from 1989 to 1998, she received more than two hundred applications each year from law schools around the country, to fill its call for "people who have demonstrated interest in public interest law or in organizing in their communities."

The third and unarguably most far-reaching addition to the Center in the 1980s was the opening of a branch office. Victor McTeer, who had clerked for Morton Stavis while in law school, had moved on to establish a law practice in Greenville, Mississippi. While serving in a volunteer capacity, he helped the CCR initiate a handful of voting rights cases. In 1984, the Center dispatched Margaret Carey to ease McTeer's burden. For many years, the Greenville office of the CCR became one of the institution's most successful operations, generating a large majority of its racial justice cases. In 2001, battered by one financial crisis after another and with its ties to the South loosening, the organization, quietly and with great regret, was forced to close the office.

Also during this time, the CCR moved its New York City headquarters from Ninth Avenue to 853 Broadway, and its continued growth was making yet another move imminent. For nearly twenty years, almost the entire time of the group's existence, Morton Stavis had been embroiled in defending Margaret and Alan McSurley from sedition charges and then suing on their behalf for damages. When the court finally awarded the McSurleys $1.6 million, Stavis contributed his fee toward buying the CCR a permanent home. The remainder of the purchase price was raised, and Floors 6 and 7 at 666 Broadway have been the Center's address since January 1, 1986. That year's *Docket Report* notes: "now that we have heat in the Winter and air conditioning in the Summer, instead of the other way around, morale has risen dramatically."

After twelve years, Marilyn Clement resigned as executive director. Her 1988 report to the board announced her decision to leave with a plaintive note: "There must be some way of working which will not emulate the power/prestige versus powerlessness/helplessness of the capitalist workplace, but that will be more responsible than our current way of working." Patricia Maher, her successor, didn't find it. Nor did Miriam Thompson, who followed Maher.

Dr. Vicki Alexander, who had joined the board of directors in 1986, became CCR co-president alongside Arthur Kinoy in 1993. Her leading role in the Rainbow Coalition had brought her into contact with Jesse Jackson associate Ron Daniels. Daniels had run for president as a third-party candidate (Peace and Freedom Party) in 1992, and had been for years closely associated with Arthur Kinoy in various movement activities. He was installed as the Center's executive director in 1994. The board's fervent hope was that in addition to restoring passion and a sense of direction for the organization, Daniels would provide strong executive leadership, something it could be argued the CCR never had, never mind how diligently Clement had tried.

The 1990s brought hard times for the CCR. A financial crisis in 1992 was the motivation for a weekend retreat. The hope was that self-examination by staff and board would solve administrative problems and refocus the work of the Center. It produced avowals of reform and a Personnel Manual. But, in fact, little changed. The Center's grip on survival was precarious.

Daniels's arrival two years later coincided with yet another money crunch. There is disagreement about whether the '94 crisis was less or more severe than the one in '92. The question is of more than academic interest; whereas the '92 emergency was met by a coming together of staff and board, the one in '94 was met by a board decree. No one questions that the '94 crisis led to developments that stunned movement people everywhere. Armed with a recommendation from Daniels, the board bypassed procedures laid down in the Personnel Manual and ordered cuts in both staff and budget. The staff, with the lone exception of Margaret Carey in Greenville, struck and joined a union. The astonishing spectacle of lawyers and legal workers picketing outside CCR headquarters continued for seven weeks.

The end of the strike left an organization with a single attorney in the New York office. Improbably, only if Center history is ignored, spirits among board and management were high and plans for the future were appropriately extravagant. Money was raised, staff was hired. Before the year was out, there was a $41 million judgment against Haitian military dictator Prosper Avril for torturing political dissidents. This was followed the next year by a decision that found Hector Gramajo, Guatemala's minister of defense, guilty of torture, assault, and false imprisonment. The CCR was back in the game.

The Center's merger in 1997 with the National Emergency Civil Liberties Committee brought new blood to the board and an infusion of funds at a time when both contributed significantly to the Center's vigor. A relentless defender of the Bill of Rights, the NECLC was founded in 1951 by a small group that included the philosopher Corliss Lamont and journalist I. F. Stone. Its executive director for almost thirty years, the late Edith Tiger, brought her organizing skills to the CCR's board, and Albert White, its office manager, moved into the same position at the Center.

Vincent Warren, a onetime Ella Baker intern, was installed as the Center's executive director on its fortieth anniversary in 2006. He'd been turned on to the organization by a Bill Kunstler speech when he was a law student at Rutgers in 1991. According to Warren, management tensions at the CCR continue to this day. There are, he said, staff lawyers in their twenties who come to the CCR from small collectively run organizations. "But we've got forty-three people, and you can't make decisions based on consensus around forty-three people. We need to be fast and we need to be reactive. And so we need to streamline our decisions."

It's a struggle confronting any group that hires people with left politics and doesn't want to conform to the standard top-down corporatist model. In ex-legal director Bill Quigley's view, the staff's union helps reduce tension by providing an outlet for staff issues. He says the decision-making process is more often by informal consultation than by seeking consensus in a structured way.

When 9/11 threw the federal government into vigorous activities said to be for the protection of the country from threats to its safety, many, including the CCR, raised the alarm that the government was too often taking actions that aren't permitted under the law. When the detention facility was opened at Guantánamo Bay for men taken captive outside the country and held as "enemy combatants," the Center was quick to file a legal challenge. The CCR's Guantánamo Global Justice Initiative pushed it to a leadership position in the fight to force the government to release internees or charge them with violations of U.S. laws. There's no question that the Center's central role in that ongoing struggle is recognized around the country. Over five hundred pro bono attorneys and law professors signed on to be trained by CCR lawyers before visiting their GITMO clients. The Initiative, says Michael Ratner, is the program he's proudest of in all the years he's been at the Center.

While the CCR still has GITMO clients, the detention center has lost the commanding position it occupied for six years. This is consistent with Center practice. "We try to go where other people have not yet gone," says Quigley, "and turn it into enough of a success that other people will be interested in doing that kind of work." The Guantánamo Initiative perfectly illustrates this principle.

With a staff of forty-three and a budget of $6.5 million, by the mid-2000s the CCR was becoming secure in the belief that it had left money crises, if not concerns, behind. Then the Bernard Madoff debacle in 2008 obliterated one of its major funding foundations and clipped the wings of others. After anxious days, other funders stepped up and a yawning hole in the 2009 budget was, in due course, filled. Plainly, there are in the community deep pockets, those devoted funders who look at the swashbuckling history of the CCR and see a bumptious band with an unorthodox approach to guarding fundamental liberties, one that is too vital to be permitted to perish.

CHAPTER 4

Kinoy

> The question of whether the case is going to be an organizing tool has to come from the movement itself, not from us, something that the movement people themselves see as an organizing tool. That means the Center has to be working side by side with movement people in every area of struggle.

The formulation is pure Arthur Kinoy. It expresses the essence of the burden he placed on his profession as he chose to style it: a "people's lawyer." A people's lawyer, the noblest calling in Kinoy's pantheon, understands that the law isn't formed, isn't finished, but rather is always and forever a work in progress. Further, a people's lawyer accepts the obligation to struggle to shape this ever-developing law to make it better serve the constituency the lawyer represents: "the people." It was Kinoy's conviction that corporate lawyers use their ready access to all levels of government to see to it that laws are passed, interpreted, and administered in the interests of the business community. Those interests are, he was equally certain, different from, and often inimical to, the interests of everyone who isn't part of that community, most notably common people. His deepest article of faith was that the people's interests are best pursued not by lawyers, not even by leaders, but by people's movements.

Attorneys who would enter the exalted ranks of Kinoy's people's lawyers place their skills and knowledge of how the system works at the service of those movements. How they do that without exploiting the deference paid them as professionals is a question Kinoy grappled with but never completely resolved.

In his review of Kinoy's autobiography, *Rights On Trial*, for *Monthly Review* magazine, Barry Winograd faulted Kinoy for not adequately coming to grips with the following problem: "given the special argumentation skills of lawyers and their privileged access to legal forums, Kinoy pays scant attention to the significant danger zone that can exist when someone is both political participant *and* legal advisor." As we shall see, it's a bum rap. He didn't solve the problem, but he certainly paid attention to it.

A primary function of a people's lawyer is to provide the nexus between a given movement and the law at the moment the two are in conflict. With the lawyer showing the way, the movement will bring a legal action against its antagonist, usually an agency of the state. The significance, the impact of the action, will be magnified by calling the public's attention to the movement and to the grievance it seeks to remedy. Increased visibility enables the movement to extend its organizing outreach. It also inserts into public discourse the issues around which the movement has organized itself.

A story has it that upon hearing CNN had arrived to cover the story of the Zapatistas in Chiapas, Mexico, at the time of the uprising of January 1994, a spokesperson for the insurgents declared: "We've won." He meant, of course, that their cause had emerged from obscurity. It was Arthur Kinoy's contention that in the United States, to achieve the same kind of victory, it isn't necessary to stage an insurrection; all you have to do is go to court.

The Center for Constitutional Rights has often been criticized by more mainstream public interest law groups for taking cases that clearly have little or no chance of prevailing if taken to court. "It depends," says David Cole, "on how you define winning and losing. If you define it solely in the courtroom, they're losing cases. If you define it more broadly, they may not be." He points out that a case, provided it has been selected with care, may ignite a wide debate.

Kinoy was adamant in holding that the Center, in deciding whether or not to take a case, must be guided by the movement. He enumerated the questions which must be asked: "Is this something the movement needs? Is this something that will develop the morale and spirit of the movement? Is this something that can be used as an educational and organizing tool for the movement?" He insisted that litigation generated by the movement rather than by lawyers will bring the odds against losing down. To the point, he said, that the most unlikely case, "if you've got sufficient support for it within the movement, you also have the possibility of winning in court."

Kinoy had no illusions about any necessary connection between justice and the courts. In his autobiography he wrote of "an underlying misconception that inevitably affects those of us seeking to integrate legal skills with political struggles." He defined the misconception as "an attitude of overreliance" on the conventional wisdom that equity, if not always perfect, is enshrined in the system by the Constitution.

Movement attorney Leonard Weinglass suggested the presence of a contradiction. The role, he said, of the federal government as the ultimate "rectifier of wrongs" was established by *Brown v. Board of Education.* Once that happened, "the way was open for Arthur Kinoy, and he moved into it beautifully."

Brown, in effect, said the court, as protector of the powerless and of minorities, has a special obligation to those communities. So perfectly did the implications of the Supreme Court's ruling premise coincide with Kinoy's political and legal philosophy, said Weinglass, that he sometimes beguiled activists with visions of the sugarplums that await at the end of the litigation trail. He had, according to Weinglass, been accused of actually defusing political movements by urging them to rely on the courts. By this reasoning, a movement reaches maturity when it is able to stage mass protests. Any lawyer who then channels that accumulated energy and experience into years-long litigation sets the movement back.

Whatever the merits of the argument, it neatly illustrates the difficulty encountered by the lawyer who purports to follow rather than lead. It's one thing to say, with Kinoy, that the impetus must come from the movement. It's another to stay on the side of the line that separates listening from speaking, heeding from directing.

Certainly Kinoy's solution to the system's tilt in favor of the wealthy and the powerful was to bring the pressure of mass movements to bear on oppressive laws by challenging them in the courts. It was why he was insistent that the impetus for litigation come from the movement rather than from the attorney. And, too, it is why he acknowledged in *Rights On Trial* a quandary as to how people's lawyers meet their responsibilities in periods "when the people's movements seem to have lost their own sense of struggle and are wholly on the defensive." He offered no clear answer.

Both of Kinoy's parents were raised in large families in the Jewish ghetto of New York City's Lower East Side. After marrying, the couple, both schoolteachers, in time settled in Brooklyn where they brought up their sons Arthur and Ernest in relative comfort. When Arthur applied for admission to Harvard, the odds against his acceptance, long enough in the best of circumstances, were multiplied many times by the quota on Jewish admissions in place at that time, as it was at most private colleges. His grandparents told him that when he got into Harvard they felt a special pride that one of their numerous family would be a schoolmate of the sons of America's elite.

William Kunstler said Kinoy was known at Harvard as "Little Lenin," little in stature, not in zeal. Kinoy enjoyed the contradictions of his undergraduate experience. He relates in *Rights On Trial* how, after rowing practice (he was the crew's coxswain), "I would leave the Morgans, the Peabodys, and the Eliots behind in the boathouse and rush up to Harvard Square to meet my friends in the office of the Student Union, where we would grab the leaflets about the next antiwar rally and start handing them out on the street."

After Harvard came three years of Second World War combat duty in North Africa and Italy. The war's end in 1945 saw Kinoy separated from the Army and on the brink of accepting a fellowship offered him by Harvard's graduate department of history. But his long-held intention to teach history was abandoned when a friend persuaded him that academia and a life devoted to political activism were incompatible. He became convinced that it really was the law that would let him, as he later wrote, "use the skills and techniques of intellectual perception directly in the daily struggle of the people."

At Columbia Law School he encountered but never became friendly with his future law partner and lifelong colleague, William Kunstler. When Kinoy graduated with the spring class in 1947, his law school record earned him an invitation from Supreme Court justice Wiley Rutledge to be interviewed for a clerkship. He was preparing to leave for Washington when word came of Rutledge's death.

Confounding the gentlemen's agreement that kept Jews out of Wall Street law firms, Kinoy was welcomed aboard by one such quite canonical firm. But Washington wasn't to be bypassed; his new employers promptly sent him to the capital to work with Frank Shea, a senior partner and former assistant secretary of the interior.

It was from Shea that Kinoy learned the lesson that came to inform so much of his career. Shea was making money for the firm's clients merely by using his familiarity with the department he had only recently administered. "Over lunch," Kinoy writes in his autobiography, "he explained to me that this was simply the way it was everywhere: there was a constant exchange back and forth between high administrative and policymaking officers in the government and personnel of the major Wall Street law firms." Along with his lunch, Kinoy digested the superb efficiency of that arrangement. It led him to develop his concept of people's lawyer as a barrier to the doctrine that "the way it was everywhere" must always and of necessity prevail. The people had been assigned the role of outsiders, while the players are leaders of financial institutions, corporations, and government. But Kinoy was certain that, using the law, the people had the power to force change on the way it is everywhere.

Kinoy had been with the firm merely three months when he received an offer to assist the general counsel of the United Electrical, Radio and Machine Workers of America, coincidentally the same union that lured Morton Stavis away from Washington. He snapped it up.

In 1948, when the Department of Justice charged the leadership of the Communist Party with conspiring to overthrow the government in violation of the terms of the Smith Act, Kinoy was just two years out of law school. Nevertheless, he wrote to the attorneys for the defendants to suggest a strategy. The government, he argued, had cited Marxist writings in bringing its case. The accused, according to the charge, were condemned by the language of their own doctrine. A defense based on trying to demonstrate that those writings don't mean what the prosecution says they mean would play into the government's hands. It implicitly concedes that the government may have a case if its interpretation of the documents in question can be shown to be correct.

Kinoy counseled the Communists to attack. They should insist that it was agents of government, not they, who were violating the law of the land by seeking to deny them their right under the First Amendment to read and write whatever they please so long as it couldn't be proved they were, in the process, placing the nation in any clear and present danger. And how to do this? By dismissing their lawyers and taking up their own defense.

Kinoy never stopped wondering if his advice wasn't heeded because the lawyers didn't want to pass up an opportunity to command center stage in a showcase trial. It's a question that haunted him, not only as it related to the Smith Act case, but to the profession generally. Do lawyers, driven by their egos, shrink from the obligation in political cases to counterattack? He searched in his autobiography into his own conflict on this score, displaying typical Arthurian chutzpah by asking if perhaps there isn't "a quality of lawyers in general that people's lawyers rarely acknowledge or face—the inner drive to obtain ego satisfaction, to dominate the scene, which often shapes their legal, tactical, and strategic decisions."

Kinoy confessed it took years of growth for him to be able to listen to opinions different from his own. He said he discovered that by suppressing urges to dismiss or condemn the ideas of others, he sometimes succeeded in enlisting in his cause more conventional attorneys as well as conservative members of the judiciary and by doing so gained effectiveness as a people's lawyer.

Kunstler cited this ability when he acknowledged it was Kinoy who taught him "never to shoot off your mouth too quickly." Constrained by Kinoy to attend "endless" meetings of movement organizations, Kunstler said he learned from his partner to keep his peace and bide his time. "He said, 'Let everyone have their say, and then formulate your own input after you've heard everyone else.' He did it very effectively." Effectively enough for civil rights leader Fannie Lou Hamer to tell Kinoy he must have been a Baptist preacher in another life.

Kunstler said he watched over the years as Kinoy, by listening instead of speaking, made people he was working with and representing feel important. He didn't, said Kunstler, "try to upstage" by taking "the usual egomaniacal lawyer's approach, that 'I know everything.'" Kunstler compared Kinoy with Stavis. "I don't think Arthur was made to be a trial lawyer, but Morty was." Kinoy was "more a theoretician, more the appellate, intellectual type. Arthur was more intellectual than Morty." He said it was Kinoy's ability to "take a team of people and whip them into a great appellate team," which, when added to Stavis's skills in court, made the CCR core group function so well together. As to the way he himself measured up to Kinoy, Kunstler dodged. "We both got divorced about the same time. We both married younger women." And finally, warmly: "I learned a lot from him."

In 1964, while working on the *Dombrowski* appeal, Kinoy was offered a tenured professorship at Rutgers School of Law. He would teach at the Constitutional Litigation Clinic. Two decades earlier he had passed up teaching in favor of a more activist life. Now he was ready to combine them; he accepted the appointment to the Rutgers Constitutional Litigation Clinic with the understanding that he would continue his practice. CCR board member Ellen Yaroshefsky remembers being ready to abandon her law studies before she took Kinoy's course. In one form or another, it's a testament often repeated. Wherever lawyers are invoking the Constitution in pursuit of social justice, it's commonplace for someone inspired and trained by Kinoy to be among them.

True to his zest for legal battle, Kinoy took on his own university when he was told in 1991 that having attained the mandatory retirement age of seventy, he had to go. He fought termination and probably surprised no one by insisting that the university's retirement rules were "totally unconstitutional." He was ultimately granted an exception and allowed to continue teaching provided outside financing could be found. The provision proved to be insurmountable, and Kinoy, having made his point, retired.

With Michael Perlin and Frank Donner, Kinoy filed the last appeal in the legal battle to save Julius and Ethel Rosenberg from execution in 1953. He was counsel to the Southern Conference Educational Fund and to Students for a Democratic Society. In 1969, he joined Kunstler and Leonard Weinglass as a member of the Chicago Seven defense team. In 1972 the Supreme Court upheld his argument that Richard Nixon had no "inherent power" as President to wiretap political organizations. He helped found the Independent Progressive Political Network in the fervent hope that it would lead to a new political formation challenging the two-party system. He was co-president of the Center for Constitutional Rights at the time of his death in September of 2003 at the age of eighty-two.

Kinoy's moment on the world stage, the moment perhaps for which the full, malignant significance of "the way it was everywhere" had been preparing him, came in 1966. The civil rights movement was in full cry, the movement against the war in Vietnam was a gathering storm, and Kinoy was thrown bodily out of a congressional hearing.

Perhaps mindful of its earlier successes harassing progressives for their supposed Communist sympathies, the House Committee on Un-American Activities was having a go at peace activists. Kinoy and Kunstler demanded the right to cross-examine a witness who was before the committee to testify against one of their clients. Kinoy, on his feet, was obstreperous in his most lawyerly fashion. The chairman banged his gavel and furiously demanded that Kinoy sit down. Kinoy continued to insist on being heard. Three federal marshals moved in, seized him and began wrestling him toward the door. "Don't touch a lawyer!" It expressed his disbelief and outrage. And then out he went, all five feet four inches of him.

A news photographer took the picture that was flashed around the world. One marshal has both hands gripped just above Kinoy's clenched fist. Another is tugging with two hands on Kinoy's other arm. The third holds Kinoy from behind with an arm locked around his throat. "The words, 'Don't touch a lawyer,'" Kinoy was to write, "triggered a sudden recognition on my part that what was happening at that moment resolved the underlying contradiction with a people's lawyer between our position in the established legal structure and our identification with the movements of fighting people."

It may be assumed that with the distinction thus erased, for one exalting if fleeting moment, Arthur Kinoy and "the people" were one.

CHAPTER 5

Stavis

Randolph Scott-McLaughlin was a young, freshly certified attorney when he presented himself at the offices of the Center for Constitutional Rights and had his first encounter with Morton Stavis. "Mort said, 'I understand you want to be a litigator.' I said, 'No, no. I want to be a trial lawyer. I'm here to work with Bill Kunstler.' 'Then you'd better know litigation.'" He stifled an objection and instead began getting up before dawn to travel by subway, then train, then bus to be in Stavis's Newark kitchen not a moment later than the appointed hour of 7:30. The young disciple would describe the cases he was preparing for the Center, while Stavis cooked breakfast and offered counsel and criticism.

Two decades later, Scott-McLaughlin paid his debt: he became a tenured professor at Pace School of Law in order to carry on his mentor's dedication to the training of young attorneys who would pursue social justice through the law.

Victor McTeer was in law school at Rutgers when he clerked for Stavis. He remembers the first time he saw Stavis in a courtroom. The Center for Constitutional Rights was not where McTeer's interests lay. Nonetheless, when Stavis asked him to help out at the Center, he agreed because it was where Stavis was spending much of his time.

"I wanted to be around him," McTeer explains. "Mort had a style, a certain kind of purity about him, and you had to be a part of that, to learn it, to understand it." He hadn't the least doubt that Stavis was the best lawyer he had ever encountered.

City University of New York law professor Frank Deale also acknowledges Stavis's influence. He describes the impact Stavis had on him when he was starting out in the law and was a new recruit on the Center's staff: "Mort was so unique because whether it was trials, appeals, Supreme Court stuff, he just had this breadth of experience about him that he could master it all." Echoing McTeer, Deale says he was certain Stavis was one of the best lawyers the United States has ever produced.

When Margaret Carey spoke about her experience as a young black CCR attorney going head to head with the white power structure in an important voting rights case in Alabama, she said it was Stavis who mentored her and gave her much-needed support while helping her find the resolve to persevere. "He just stayed with me, stayed with me . . . and we took it to its conclusion."

That each of these enthusiasts is African American is significant. Respect for Stavis's abilities, of course, isn't limited to any single constituency. When a trial lawyer with as many notches on his gun as William Kunstler called Stavis "a very effective courtroom lawyer," it's lavish praise. Nancy Stearns said he was "one of the most skilled lawyers, both appellate and trial, that I have ever known." Still, expressions of approval from young black attorneys add to the evidence that Stavis took special pains to shepherd African Americans when they began to show up on the Center's roster of staff attorneys at the end of the1970s. David Cole, who is white and arrived in that period, says he was aware that Stavis offered more of his time and assistance to minority lawyers. "He was a mentor for Randy Scott-McLaughlin, for example, but not for me."

His friendship in the late 1950s with Martin Luther King was instrumental in moving Stavis into an active role in the civil rights movement. It was as a Jew that he discovered in that struggle a special resonance. According to McTeer, Stavis was, if not a Zionist in any formal sense, certainly a Jewish nationalist. McTeer recalls walks home from the office with Stavis during which the older man probed for commonalities in the respective histories of blacks and Jews. Once, he insisted he saw similarities between Theodore Herzl and Malcolm X. McTeer says Stavis believed the Holocaust resonated in the liberation fight of African Americans and looked upon these experiences as an irrevocable bond linking the respective cultures. The unity of blacks and Jews, says George Stavis, was his father's "great driving force."

From his position of intense involvement in the civil rights movement, it was painful for Stavis to watch certain black leaders discover in anti-Semitic demagogy an easy route to the rewards of notoriety. It made him regard efforts then surfacing at the CCR to find ways to aid the Palestinian cause in the Middle East with even more wariness than he might otherwise. On his website, Ben Stavis notes that his father never represented a Palestinian charged with terror. George Stavis remembers "dark moments" when his father sensed that pro-Arab sensibilities among some CCR staff people had as a correlative, if not an anti-Semitic, certainly an anti-Israel bias.

The question arises: How would Stavis have responded in 2001 when the Center was wrestling with the thorny issue of should it initiate an action that could lead to representing Muslims accused of being terrorists? David Cole recalls that when he brought the Los Angeles Eight case to the Center—eight Palestinians threatened with deportation—"Morty was hesitant."

Not that he adjusted his standards to suit skin color. "You had to have an ego to deal with Mort," said McTeer. "You had to keep up. He was a very progressive guy on the one hand, but on the other hand his view of clerks was very old school. You carried a briefcase for Mort. And it was a while before you gained his respect. If you put out an idea that wasn't particularly bright or brilliant, he'd just move right by you like you weren't there."

Deale remembers that the first time he worked with Stavis he took exception to a standard Stavis practice. He was asked to put together an appendix on an appeal Stavis was preparing. Deale says, "That's really a paralegal task, and I refused to do it." It surely is a measure of the man that Stavis never made Deale pay for his insurrection. "We had this struggle in the beginning, but once we began to understand each other, it was an amazing experience working with him."

Scott-McLaughlin, on the other hand, was content from the time he arrived at the CCR to perform infra dig chores for Stavis in exchange for the opportunity to learn from the best. He'd have been "a fool not to take advantage of what those guys could teach me," he says in a reference to the CCR's founding elders.

"He trained the young lawyers" was the way Kunstler explained Stavis's role when, in 1969, the Center became, with greater deliberation, an educational as well as legal formation.

Teaching, of course, is as universally avoided as it is held in esteem. At the same time as he was tending to a practice and helping raise a family, Stavis undertook to become an adjunct law professor at Seton Hall and at Rutgers. As a teacher, it wasn't unknown for him to overreach. He enjoyed the role of mentor but didn't easily accept having his tutelage questioned.

Former staff attorney Elizabeth Schneider believes it was often hard for Stavis not to be impatient with still-developing skills and ideas about how to use them. "Morty was a very strong person," says Schneider. "He was extremely smart and talented. But he absolutely had his own particular way of seeing things. It was frequently a wonderful experience to work with him, because it was stimulating and taught you a lot. But it was easier the less experienced you were, because then it was more sitting at the feet of someone. As you developed your own independent ideas and agendas, sometimes he was very respectful of that and appreciative and helpful, and sometimes he wasn't."

It was the period in the 1970s when the Center's docket, as we've seen, had become dominated to a significant degree by work being done by women attorneys, largely in the area of women's rights. It could not have been easy for Stavis to watch his beloved CCR take up with so much vigor a cause with which he felt so uncomfortable. When confronted with Stavis's objections, Schneider says she felt "the way you might about a father you were pissed at." The comparison becomes especially apt when she and others speak of the affection they received from Stavis and readily returned.

Nancy Stearns had difficulties with Stavis that mirror Schneider's. "Morty made everybody his kid," Stearns contends. "It was a struggle with Morty to get you from being his child to being somebody who was a real lawyer."

Surely at least part of Stavis's problem was that the staff often had credentials but little else to qualify them as litigators as he understood the term. He knew how raw they were. They, of course, had to have known, as well. What triggered occasional tension is that many chose to bluff it out.

Because the women were trailblazers, breaking ground in women's law, they thought they were leaving their mentor behind. "The truth is," Stearns acknowledges with the benefit of time's passage, "we clearly weren't equal to him. . . . We demanded equal respect we weren't entitled to."

Charges of paternalism were never leveled by male lawyers taking instruction from Stavis. Entitled or not, the young women could no more withdraw their demands for respect than Stavis could stop telling them what to do and how to do it.

It was an irrepressible conflict, with the staff, by Stearns's account, finding it "incredibly hard to get over that hump to where we weren't treated as children."

The question that then insists upon intruding is, was there a sexist component lurking in Stavis's paternalism? A clue to the answer may be located in the fact that of the men questioned for this book, none reported being treated by Stavis as a child. Nor were charges of paternalism ever leveled by male lawyers taking instruction from Stavis. By David Cole's account, for example, Stavis took care to use neither his age nor wisdom to dominate the dynamic of the group.

"Morty had a lot of influence, but it was relatively subtle. He wasn't someone who was overseeing people. He was a good facilitator. In staff meetings, he was one of the people. It really was very collective." Volunteer staff attorney Ralph Shapiro agrees. He remembers Stavis listening "with an open mind to the opinions of others," even as he acknowledges Stavis's "tremendous self-confidence and ego."

There can be no question that Stavis's natural inclination was to insist that his way was the right way. It becomes, then, all the more remarkable that he would often startle people by repositing an entirely unwarranted confidence in them. Once Frank Deale asserted his independence, for instance, Stavis accepted him unequivocally as a co-counsel. Deale remembers going with Stavis to take a deposition. He had never conducted one, but when they got into the room Stavis told him to get started. "I was five minutes into the deposition, and he left. That was his style." Similarly, Scott-McLaughlin credits Stavis with helping him enter a courtroom long before he felt up to the task. "Don't be intimidated when you're up against a big law firm," he recalls Stavis telling him. "By hard work you can do what they can do and do it better because you believe in what you're doing." And when Mark Amsterdam wasn't sure his experience qualified him to charge off to Okinawa, it was primarily Stavis who assured him it would be a piece of cake.

As the lead lawyer in the appeal of the contempt citations issued to the attorneys in the Chicago Seven case, Stavis organized a campaign to have lawyers around the country write memos on various aspects of contempt law. Assisted by James Reif, Stavis culled the memos that poured in for the arguments on which they built their successful brief. Contempt was an issue that preoccupied Stavis. He knew lawyers needed to be creative in their defense of activists charged with contempt if they had any hope of prevailing. For courts to then hold the attorneys themselves in contempt or hit them with Rule 11 sanctions (arguments that are "frivolous" or have no "evidentiary support") was dirty pool.

It struck him as unjust that judges should protect government policy from those who would challenge it by attacking the lawyers representing the challengers. He brought spirited defenses to Rule 11 sanctions until the rule was revised to make it less restrictive, and its use was largely abandoned.

For the first decade of the CCR's life, Stavis clearly yielded to his propensity for taking charge. The Center, as his widow, Esther, put it to me, was "his baby." It isn't hard to understand why he would be inclined to impose not only his values and standards but his methods as well. Of that period, Kunstler said, he, Smith, and Kinoy "were the dreamers." It was Stavis "who knew enough about civil law to put this together."

Stavis's contribution to the success of the CCR is a matter of record and wide acknowledgment. In the years before the organization formalized its structure, Stavis shouldered so many administrative functions that Robert Boehm conceded he was for all practical purposes the organization's executive director. Elizabeth Schneider contends he also performed duties customarily assigned to a legal director. "He was the person who if you really weren't sure about what to do you'd call." Stavis, she adds, was "the glue, the major older person who was there who could function as a litigation director. Arthur [Kinoy] was in and out . . . Bill [Kunstler] wasn't capable of functioning that way, and Peter [Weiss)] had his own firm. Having the benefit of Morty's history and insight and experience was an enormous strength of the Center." Such, she believes, was his contribution, that his death in 1992 left the Center with a cavity at its core that required years of struggle to fill. In Schneider's summation: "It was a combination of his lawyering capacity, his very deep commitment to the Center as an institution, the amount of time and energy he put into it. . . . He was clearly the one who had the major responsibility for the Center's growth and success."

William Kunstler was equally persuaded that Stavis was, if not sufficient to the task of maintaining the Center's vigor, at least necessary to it. "He was successful in bringing in money, publicizing the organization, [and] litigating the case [*McSurley*] that got us the money to buy the two floors." When Stavis died, Kunstler believed the CCR wouldn't survive. "I thought after Morton's death the Center wouldn't be able to attract funding and would decline. That it continued is a total tribute to Morton Stavis. He was the spirit and guiding hand."

President and ex-legal director Michael Ratner believes the board–staff confrontation of October 1994 might have occurred but not in the same way had Stavis been alive. He says had Stavis been on hand there would not have been a picket line in the street. "Ever, ever, ever. It would have never happened. The worst that would have happened would have been wholesale departures."

Stavis was born Moishe Isaac Stavisky in 1915 in New York City. His father, who worked in the garment business, was an Orthodox Jew who allowed his son to grow up outside the strict codes of that sect. (McTeer attributes Stavis's considerable brief-writing skills to his early training in the Talmud.) There was no family history of left politics;

instead, George Stavis locates his father's political development in the Depression-fueled ferment on the City College of New York campus. As he became radicalized, he abandoned formal religious observance, but never his family and never his Jewish identity. He enrolled in Columbia University's School of Law, made law review and graduated with the class of 1936. It was his identity as a Jew that closed to Stavis career opportunities with leading New York law firms.

Franklin Roosevelt's first term was coming to an end. Washington was alive with bold ideas being hammered into legislation. Spurned by New York City's elite corporate club, Stavis saw in the New Deal, if not a cornucopia of opportunity, at least a port in a storm. He found a job with the Federal Security Agency in Washington, D.C.

Still short of his twenty-second birthday, he threw himself into his first case: the defense of the constitutionality of the Social Security Act that obligated the federal government, for the first time in its history, to ensure that Americans might live with a modicum of dignity after they stopped working. The law survived the test despite a distraction visited upon one of its defenders: Stavis's encounter with Esther Auerbach, an economist at the SSA, culminated in their marriage two years later.

By his second year in Washington, Stavis was acclimated enough to welcome challenges beyond his government employment. He helped Robert Kenny found the National Lawyers Guild and became active in the union that organized federal employees. The union brought him the first case he ever litigated on his own, a successful suit to reinstate a black government attorney whose firing forced the issue of racism into public scrutiny. His course was set.

Stavis's work for the union also brought him to the attention of one of Washington's heaviest hitters: New York's senator, Robert F. Wagner. Wagner had been the principal author of the National Labor Relations Act. Known as the Wagner Act, the law was hailed as the Magna Carta of labor. It was called a "great leap forward" for unions. In truth it was designed primarily to fuel the depressed economy. If unions were strong enough, the theory went, disposable income in the pockets of working people would mean happy days would be here again. And, in fact, after the act's passage, union organizing flourished. Supporters in the Senate argued that passage of the resolution, by replacing the welter of local labor regulations with a federal law, would smooth interstate commerce. Wagner took the twenty-three-year-old Stavis on as a legislative assistant.

Labor leaders didn't care about the reasons government encouraged them. Their time had come, and they adored Wagner. Caught in their warm embrace was the senator's young assistant, Morton Stavis. With the end of the Second World War in 1945, Stavis was ready to leave government and accept the blandishments of the United Electrical Workers, who dispatched him to represent its locals in New Jersey. He brought with him Margaret Thompson from the union's headquarters. She would be his lifelong secretary.

Morton and Esther and their sons Benedict, George, and Robert settled in Elizabeth, New Jersey in 1945. George remembers the lengths his mother went to keep the family from being isolated in an era defined by the emerging Cold War. She became a Cub Scout den mother and involved herself in the activities of the local Jewish community.

George Stavis says his father was acutely conscious of the way, given the tenor of the times, that his activities exposed him and his family to being stigmatized. He saw to it that his movement work was as quietly consultative as he could keep it and avoided leadership roles. Even so, both he and Esther were called to Washington to testify before the House Committee on Un-American Activities about their political associations.

Stavis was denounced on the Senate floor by Mississippi's senator Eastland. He became especially marked when, during the anticommunist hysteria in the early 1950s, he defended a United Auto Workers organizer accused of sedition. George remembers his father going to work with an escort, one car ahead and one car behind. At home he and his brothers had "a 350-pound babysitter for security."

The Stavis family always had a welcoming spare bedroom, even after they moved to an apartment in Newark. When Victor McTeer didn't have enough money to remain in law school, Morton and Esther took him in, and he became known as the fourth Stavis brother. "You've got to remember this is Newark in 1971," McTeer says. "Black-white relationships aren't exactly stellar. So here's this Jewish family with this big black kid coming in and out. It raised eyebrows in the building, but it raised more eyebrows at Rutgers which was the heartland of radical left thinking. And not especially integration thinking. Morty and I both caught heat, but that's one of the things that made the relationship very strong."

McTeer says Stavis once confided to him the biggest regret of his career: he never became a judge. Another regret he told me about was that he never sailed his forty-one-foot ketch across the Atlantic. He made one attempt. With the Talmudic meticulousness he devoted to his briefs, he planned and plotted over many months. Equipment and provisions were exactingly selected and fastidiously stowed. The great adventure began. Within days the vessel was battered by a violent storm. Esther, who topped out at less than five feet and weighed correspondingly little, issued an edict: they were turning around and going home. The skipper put the wheel over.

As the CCR inevitably altered its character, Stavis's position in it became more peripheral. It was, as George concedes, "his baby," as his mother had styled it, but like babies do it had grown into something that was not quite in the image he had of it. Even so, he refused to be pushed aside.

In 1983, Stavis closed his firm in Newark and moved his office into the Center. When the new Aquino government of the Philippines approached the CCR in 1986 about helping it recover billions in assets expropriated by Ferdinand Marcos, Stavis told the staff that if they accepted the case he and voluntary attorneys Ralph Shapiro and Mahlon Perkins would do the work. He devoted himself to the case almost full-time for three years.

Then, in 1989, Stavis finally collided head-on with the Center staff. He was stunned when they refused to let him run the appeal of the Margaret Kelly Michaels daycare case through the Center. Moving his office to a room in his apartment, he worked almost obsessively on the brief until his death.

Esther Stavis said that toward the end of his career her husband often voiced regret that so many of the young people coming to work at the Center straight from law school "wanted to go off in all directions" and turned to him with decreasing frequency. Former legal director Michael Deutsch thinks the problem was primarily generational. The new lawyers "had a lot of P.C.-type politics, so that if they didn't agree with Morty on every issue under the sun, then they weren't able to get the great experience and brilliance of the lawyer that he was, and they went off into their own thing." Frank Deale attributes the staff's increasing rejection of Stavis to what he called immaturity and egotism. "I was the last one of my generation to go to him," he said. "I came to love him. I can't tell you the vacuum I felt after he died."

Stavis was honored in 1974 for his contribution to civil liberties by the American Civil Liberties Union of New Jersey. Kunstler, making the presentation, said the body of Stavis's work was "like the political-economic history of the American people over the past forty years." Stavis, he said, had been involved in "every critical constitutional issue facing the nation."

CHAPTER 6

Kunstler

The law is hidden in the stately books
That line the lawyers' inner wall.
Just waiting for the lucky searcher's hooks
To find the precedent that conquers all.
"We build upon the past," the scholars say,
"And what some court said many years ago
May well decide the fate of one today,
Or tell which party has the right to crow."
The law clerks leaf through volumes by the score
To seek the clue the partners hope is there,
So that they find the winning law before
The other side has stripped the cupboard bare.
Each nugget found in such a paper mine
Is more than worth its weight in billing time.

Along with the pleasure he took in skewering the law with his sonnets, some unpublished like this one, William

Moses Kunstler liked to quote Shakespeare's *King Henry VI, Part II*: "The first thing we do, let's kill all the lawyers." He heeded the spirit if not the letter of that injunction by having as little as possible to do with the prosecutors trying to convict his clients in criminal trials. "I don't talk to them unless I have to and then only on a very professional level. I don't shake hands, I don't palsy around. Knowing how much prosecutorial misconduct they engage in, I stay totally aloof."

In his later years, Kunstler came to regard the institution of the law with a contempt that he openly, almost proudly, proclaimed. He declared himself not an officer of the court, but of his client. He liked to think of himself as standing squarely in the path of abusive government, "fighting to keep people alive, literally, or to keep them out of jail, or to preserve their forums. . . ."

Kunstler traced this harsh judgment of the justice system to his defense of anti-Vietnam War activists in Chicago in 1969. In point of fact, he began practicing law with something less than enthusiasm. His younger brother, Michael, enrolled in Columbia Law School at the time William was being separated from the army at the end of the Second World War. William claimed to have mindlessly followed Michael's lead without any intention of actually becoming a lawyer. He said, "I only went to law school out of sibling rivalry."

In *My Life as a Radical Lawyer*, his autobiography written with Sheila Isenberg, Kunstler said it was while he was in law school that his disinterest gave way to a conviction that the law can be a "powerful force for justice, the only equitable method available to people for correcting wrongs." He remained persuaded throughout his first twenty years in the profession that violations of rights by agencies of government are aberrations, and that that is why courts and lawyers are central to the system—to restore the balance when the scales of justice get tipped by overzealous or unprincipled officials.

Born in 1919 to Fanny and Dr. Monroe Kunstler, the young Bill was seldom out of trouble. "In many ways," he wrote, "I am still that little boy who always must act outrageously so he can remain outside the mainstream."

Kunstler, however, wasn't so far out of the mainstream that he wouldn't or couldn't enroll as an undergraduate in Yale University, and then in Columbia University's School of Law. He was admitted to the bar in 1948 and promptly opened an office with his brother. He listed his name with the American Civil Liberties Union, to be called on as and when the need arose, and settled into the firm's general practice and to teaching a course on trusts and estates at New York Law School, none remotely an outrageous act.

William Worthy was a journalist whose passport was taken away following a forbidden visit to China. In 1956 his was Kunstler's first civil rights case. That he permitted four years to pass before he undertook another—Caryl Chessman's unsuccessful appeal of his death sentence in California—would seem to support his description of himself as a "parlor liberal."

In 1961, Kunstler found himself beginning to be pushed out of the parlor and into the tempest of the civil rights struggle. Push truly came to shove when the ACLU asked him to swing by Jackson, Mississippi, on his way home from a trip to the West Coast. His assignment was "to tell Jack Young, a black lawyer down there, that the ACLU stands behind him. Young said, 'Fuck all that, I need lawyers here.'"

It was the early days of the Freedom Riders, and Young knew any contingent arriving in his support would be met by the police. He told Kunstler to go downtown to the Greyhound bus station and do whatever he could. The group that got off the bus was made up of blacks and whites. They walked into the station and were promptly arrested and taken to the state penitentiary. Kunstler remembers this as a transformative moment. He wrote that as he left the bus station "I said, 'By God, I'm going to stay.'"

Kunstler began spending more time in Mississippi than at home. "I met Martin [Dr. Martin Luther King, Jr.] for the first time, and he asked me if I would consider being his special trial counselor." King asked him to step into the case of sixteen-year-old Thomas Wansley who had been sentenced to death in Virginia for rape. Kunstler knew Arthur Kinoy had helped defend a black man accused of rape in Alabama. He enlisted Kinoy in the Wansley case. When they won the appeal, Kunstler interested Kinoy in "going around the South with me for Martin King."

"We went everywhere," Kunstler said, "and we became very close and tight." He remembered a law student who dubbed him and Kinoy "The Messiah and the Great K." They never figured out which was which.

In 1963, Kunstler and Kinoy decided to formalize their relationship and the new firm of Kunstler, Kunstler, and Kinoy was launched. Kunstler said Kinoy delighted in referring to them, especially to southern judges, as "the new KKK." In spite of what Kinoy called "enormous differences between us," he and Kunstler were oddly complementary. "Bill Kunstler had a drive and self-confidence that led him unhesitatingly into the center of the fray, sometimes without a thought-out plan or strategy," Kinoy wrote in his autobiography. These qualities, when combined with Kinoy's devotion to planning and preparation, made the two what Kinoy was pleased to call "a powerful team."

It was a time tailored to Kunstler's outsized dimensions. Excitement was in the air, the attention of the country was increasingly on the work he and other civil rights lawyers were doing; in sum, the law was his mistress, beguiling and modestly rewarding and generous in providing opportunities for ego gratification. "We were winning all the time," Kunstler remembered. "All you had to do was make a good record. You had the federal government with you. You were fighting the rednecks in the Deep South." What could be more satisfying or exalting? Then came the Chicago Seven trial.

Kunstler had lived half a century secure in the conviction that the government of the United States was not the same as other governments. It would, no matter what the provocation, play by the rules. In the course of the trial of the Chicago Seven, Kunstler came to believe absolutely that he was watching United States attorneys and a federal judge lie and deceive and distort those same rules beyond recognition in order to convict seven men of the vague crime of conspiring. His inamorata, the law, turned while still clasped in his embrace into a succubus. "I was taught how dirty the government is, how vicious it is, and how overpowering it can be when it's after certain people."

He felt betrayed. The bitterness never left him. He spent the rest of his life an avowed enemy of the state. "Chicago was my rebirth. I had found my place in the world." At the end of the tempestuous trial, Kunstler was charged with twenty-four counts of contempt of court.

"There is no other lawyer in the country that could have handled this case the way Bill Kunstler did," said his co-

counsel Leonard Weinglass. "And that is principally a question of courage." Weinglass said there were times when Kunstler told him he knew what he was about to say would draw a contempt citation, but it had to be said, and then he would stand and say it. "Now, very few lawyers would do that, but Bill did." One result of Kunstler's confrontational behavior in the Chicago trial, said Weinglass, is the impact it had on law students. "When I met young lawyers then who were in law school and getting out, they all wanted to be Bill Kunstler. By that they meant lawyers who would stand up to abuse of authority in the courtroom. And so Bill really had an impact on the practice of law and the practice of young lawyers."

After Chicago, Kunstler declined to style himself a civil libertarian in any conventional sense of the term. His experience there was so alienating that ever after the law was his sworn enemy: "the law and those who administer it, whether they are law enforcement or judicial or wardens or whatever." It came ultimately to be how he justified defending some of society's most despised pariahs: Larry Davis, a notorious drug dealer; El Sayyid A. Nosair, no sooner acquitted of assassinating the fiery rabbi Meir Kahane then accused of helping to bomb the World Trade Center; Yusef Salaam, convicted (and later exonerated) of attacking and raping and maiming a young woman jogger in New York City's Central Park; and Colin Ferguson, who indiscriminately gunned down passengers on a Long Island Railroad commuter train.

The inventory goes on like a roll call of the damned. When the northern New Jersey *Record* said Kunstler could be found "at the eye of nearly every prominent left-wing or civil rights hurricane" for a decade or more following

Chicago, this was indisputably true. His indelible identification with movement causes and activists certainly remained in 1971 when prisoners took over the Attica Correctional Facility in upstate New York and held guards hostage. It was to Kunstler they turned to negotiate for them and speak for them to the outside world. It was Kunstler who was summoned by the American Indian Movement to the Pine Ridge Reservation during the siege of Wounded Knee in the winter of 1972–73. In time, though, the hurricanes increasingly had little or no left connection. Kunstler's rationale for charging into them was that he accepted clients when he believed they were "being oppressed," but it ultimately became difficult for him to define "oppression" with any precision. If the state is an oppressor, must it not follow that anyone accused of criminal activity by the state is, virtually by definition, a victim of oppression?

Few clients could be more unloved than the two men charged with bombing the World Trade Center in 1993. Until the judge removed him on a technicality, Kunstler vigorously took up the cause of defendants Siddig Ibrahim Siddig Ali and Ibrahim El-Gabrowny. He hadn't the least doubt that, because the accused were alleged to be Islamists, they were victims of official misconduct. "The government," he said, was "really going after these people." It was going to "rip them apart." The case thus became for Kunstler an opportunity, having nothing in the least to do with the guilt or innocence of the accused, but of challenging the government.

Some say Kunstler's choice of clients often indicated that he'd lost his way. Lynne Stewart, a movement lawyer who once worked closely with Kunstler, acknowledges that he became involved in cases that were less than "pure." Since offering that judgment, Stewart has herself been convicted of improper procedure while representing a Moslem cleric accused in a terrorist bombing. Attorney Alan Dershowitz attributes Kunstler's remarkable rogue's gallery of clients to the simple fact that he "ran out of causes."

Had there been truth in that assessment, it would have been reflected in Kunstler's diminishing relevance and influence, something that never happened. He continued until his death in September 1995 to inspire lawyers and young people to, as *The New York Times* put it, "take up public interest work and to defend clients whom most other lawyers would shun." Demand for his services, even among perfectly orthodox people charged with crimes, remained steady throughout his career.

There wasn't always perfect consistency in the tests Kunstler applied to clients. Whereas no crime was too vile to get a petitioner turned away at Kunstler and Kuby (Ronald L. Kuby was Kunstler's last law partner), incorrect politics could, in the absence of other considerations, slam the door. "The person whose politics are right of center," Kunstler explained, "we don't take. As to non-political people, we take those we think are being oppressed."

Most of his clients were people of color. He defined his role as "fighting fire with fire, shamelessly, on behalf of my clients." All he needed to know was that no matter how despicable the people he represented, if the time ever came to go to the barricades, they'd show up on his side. With that knowledge, he had the justification he required to represent them with vigor, his critics be damned.

Kunstler used as an office a small room on the garden-level floor of his Georgian house in New York's Greenwich Village. Ron Kuby worked out of an adjacent room the size of a small scullery. Their secretaries made do in a hallway at the foot of narrow stairs leading to the home above where Kunstler lived with his wife, Margaret Ratner. All doors were left open. Interoffice communication was by holler. Kunstler conducted his business at a scarred, ornate table that bore a personal computer, lamp, telephone, untidy files and piles of paper.

After his immersion in criminal law following the Chicago Seven case, Kunstler began to question the relevance of the CCR. It was the opinion of former CCR staff attorney Beth Stephens that Kunstler came to view Center cases as not particularly useful politically. Indeed, Kunstler said he had often thought of separating himself from the group. He said he believed the Center's board of directors made a mistake in letting the organization "degenerate into a collective." He believed a result was that civil litigation took precedence over criminal cases. It did simply because the staff attorneys controlled which cases the Center would take, and they had little or no experience in trying criminal cases. Given that the system, in Kunstler's view, weighs most heavily on those who are accused of crimes, he believed the Center's emphasis on bringing civil actions wasn't the most effective use of the organization's resources. He said it was all right to have all "these civil rights actions for all sorts of causes, and they're all to the good, but there is that area of the criminal law where the crunch goes on every day and where probably the most harm is done, and the Center doesn't enter. We don't have a real criminal law setup over there. That's a weakness."

"Where the most harm is done" is the key to understanding how Kunstler wanted to function as an attorney after Chicago. He was persuaded that the state condemns a great many of its citizens to the humiliation and degradation of poverty and the oppression attendant on membership in a racial minority and then criminalizes them when, by one means or another, they renounce the role assigned to them. By defending these dissenters in court, he believed he was being as effective a counterpoise to the state as the law permitted.

One result was he was frequently at odds with the CCR staff over cases he brought in. Those cases—the "crazy cases" as he called them—he then undertook to defend on his own, accepting the hard circumstance that the accused were often indigent. With becoming candor, he compared himself to Don Quixote in the sense that there were times when he "mistook windmills for the real quarry."

Mark Amsterdam recalls sharing Kunstler's frustration with the Center when he was a staff attorney in the early 1970s. "Bill and I believed in the criminal side, to protect the liberty of those who'd been organizing, fighting. . . . There was an immediacy there."

Yet Kunstler, for better or worse, kept his Center connection and remained on the board of directors. However problematic that connection was for him, it was at times no less so for others. In the early years, Kunstler's celebrity could often be a burden the staff bore with exasperation. Rhonda Copelon remembered the start of many a telephone conversation: "'Is this Bill Kunstler's office?' 'No, this is the Center for Constitutional Rights.' We had to work to establish the identity of CCR and its staff." In 1985, the *San Diego Tribune* referred to Ronald Kuby as "an associate of Kunstler's New York based Center for Constitutional Rights." A 1987 Kunstler profile in the *Boston Globe* called him "head of the Center for Constitutional Rights." A headline on a *Chicago Sun-Times* article about the Center's campaign against the nomination of Robert Bork to the Supreme Court reads, "Kunstler Group Prepares to Fight Top Court Choice."

On the other hand, Janice Goodman found Kunstler's celebrity useful when she was a staff attorney in the 1970s. "Now you say, 'I work at the Center for Constitutional Rights' and whole groups of people know who you are. In those days, you'd have to say, 'You know, the organization Bill Kunstler is with.'" Former executive director Marilyn Clement said the media attention Kunstler drew to the Center was "sometimes good, sometimes bad." Name recognition when calling on people to contribute money was good. Donors outraged by Kunstler's latest client, even when it wasn't a Center case, was bad.

Then too, there were times when seeing to it that their loose cannon didn't go overboard kept all hands on deck. Speaking of the early seventies, former staff attorney James Reif says there was "a whole cottage industry representing Bill. He was always getting into trouble. . . . Contempt was a serious problem in those days."

Kunstler was out of step with the Center in other ways. For example, fault lines inevitably appeared when women's rights overtook civil rights and antiwar activity as a dominant concern. As we've seen, he wasn't alone in believing the organization he'd help found was going perilously off course. He was, however, conspicuously absent among those who labored to help the office create space for women and women's law. Elizabeth Schneider believes the Center made the transition with less difficulty than many similar groups were able to manage in a time of so much ferment because "everybody who was there—Bill being an exception—was committed to the Center and its survival as an institution and to its importance."

There is evidence, too, that even more than the other seniors, Kunstler used the Center as a way of getting bright young attorneys to do some of his work for him. No one doubted his talent. On his feet in a courtroom, he had an ability not often matched by opposing lawyers to persuade jurors. It was the preparation for that moment when he could shine that he had little patience. He was good at generating ideas on which to base a defense but often couldn't be bothered doing the research that would give foundation to his ideas. As Schneider puts it, "Bill never subjected himself to the collective experience in the sense of participating in meetings or sense of responsibility. He was always sort of off somewhere. When he had a case that basically he wanted the Center to pay for, he would come in and present it as a Center case. Or if he wanted help on it or he thought there'd be an advantage in terms of PR, he'd bring it in."

Ex-legal director Frank Deale was another who said he saw Kunstler exploit the Center. He confirms that when his cases required research and writing, Kunstler liked to have others take on the burden of those chores. Deale characterizes Kunstler as "a good lawyer on his feet in a courtroom before a jury. He'd come to a staff meeting and he had a way of establishing eye contact, and he had this voice. . . . He could be telling you a jaw full of lies, but you'd believe him." Len Weinglass was more forthright in his reservations about Kunstler's courtroom skill: "Flamboyance has a place and can also be inappropriate."

David Cole describes Kunstler as very likeable and charming. His strengths, Cole says, were "talking to ordinary people about justice, to juries, cross-examination." He was colorful and smart and light on his feet. But when it came to the hard work of preparing for court appearances, Cole says, Kunstler wasn't to be relied upon, even on cases of transcendent importance. He recalls working together on the 1989 and 1990 flag burning cases: "I basically wrote the briefs and he didn't do anything." It was the client, Gregory Lee Johnson, who decreed that the argument in front of the Supreme Court should be made by Kunstler.

As the butt of an old joke at the Center, Kunstler might have been expected to be vexed by it but in fact loved to tell it. It went: If Arthur Kinoy asks you to write a brief, he reads it and says, "This is the greatest thing I've ever seen in my life! Wonderful, wonderful! Let's just go through it and see what it needs." If Mort Stavis asks you to do a brief, he reads it and says, "This is the shittiest thing I've ever read. We've got to get started rewriting it." If Bill Kunstler asks you to do a brief, you hand it to him and he says, "Where do I sign?" He acknowledged the joke's essential truth with the explanation that if someone is trained and accredited, he took it for granted that they were competent in what he considered the craft of the law. To Kunstler, the art of the law is in the passion and conviction a lawyer conveys to a jury.

But if Kunstler did in fact use the Center, he was used as well. Randolph Scott-McLaughlin says he pegged Kunstler as "one of the great trial lawyers" and joined the CCR in part to learn from him. He persuaded Kunstler to mentor him by telling him, "You owe me." When asked why, the younger man explained it was Kunstler, in an address to his class at Harvard, who told the law students that just as white attorneys had taken in race prejudice with their mothers' milk, so did black lawyers come with an inherited obligation to get into the fight for human rights and justice. It was that message, Scott-McLaughlin told Kunstler, which brought him to the CCR. "Bill agreed to take me under his wing."

A 1994 article in *The New York Times* called Kunstler "arguably the most recognizable lawyer in the United States." When he was spotted on the street, the article went on, he was often cursed or excoriated as a self-hating Jew. *Vanity Fair* called him the most hated lawyer in America.

Kunstler preferred to regard his celebrity another way. "It's nice to be known all over. People shout from cars, 'Go get 'em!'" With recognition, he said, come more cases, and with more cases come more exciting cases. He once told *The Boston Globe* he used publicity as "an indispensable political tool." He went on to assert his conviction that it's through the media that you get people to pay attention, to become concerned.

The cavernous Cathedral of St. John the Divine in uptown Manhattan was standing room only for Kunstler's 1995 memorial service. Michael Ratner read from a valedictory Kunstler had written to be opened after his death. It said: "If I had the opportunity to live my life all over again, I do not believe that I would change a thing except, perhaps, some of my more flamboyant utterances. I have hardly lived a life of quiet desperation but one filled with a plethora of high points that more than compensated for those that fell below the line. . . . So goodbye to everyone, named and unnamed, who filled my days with delight, accomplishment, and satisfaction. You do not need me to remind you that the struggle to attain and maintain human liberty and to resist oppression and tyranny is the perennial obligation of all who understand its necessity, and the only memorial that I require is your solemn determination to remain on the ramparts and barricades until, like me, you pass into the great scheme of things."

Kunstler liked to quote Oliver Wendell Holmes on one's duty "to share the passion and action of our times" when driving home his impatience with movement attorneys who grow disheartened and leave the field. "To leave the law, turn away from it when you've got that ticket and you've got good instincts and principles, I think is terrible." The "ticket" for Kunstler was access to the tribunal of a courtroom. "We can't get in the Oval Office, we can't get on the floor of Congress, but we can get these forums, and I use them shamelessly."

A year before he died he welcomed me to his cubby of an office on Gay Street. He leaned back in his chair, contemplated his dogs harassing each other at his feet. "If these cases were boring to me, I wouldn't be as good as I am and I wouldn't like it as much as I do. We're not Galahads who have the strength of ten because my heart is pure—our hearts are not so pure—but because we get a kick out of it. It's fun. You've got to like what you're doing, and I can't think of anything I like better than this. Excitement . . . notoriety . . . I wake up every morning and say, 'It's going to be an exciting day.' "

CHAPTER 7

Smith

Young staffers at the CCR refer to him as "the lost founder." Stavis, Kunstler, and Kinoy are legendary, but who was Ben Smith?

When state police officers kicked in the door of a small New Orleans law office on an October afternoon in 1963, they made a mess, confiscated files, and obliged the state of Louisiana to bite off more than it was ultimately going to be able to chew. The raid led to court battles. The battles led to the state being constrained to change the way it protected its citizens from enemies both foreign and domestic.

The proprietor of the raided office, Benjamin Smith, was arrested at home later the same day. His alleged crime was that he was subversive and hence a threat to the ability of the state to preserve itself. The state's evidence against Smith was based on abundant and unconcealed proof of his affiliations with subversive organizations, which they claimed was made clear by the files seized during their raid. Smith was hauled to the lockup.

James Dombrowski, executive director of the Southern Conference Educational Fund (SCEF), had been picked up earlier in the same sweep. It's not unlikely that when Smith showed up at the jail, Dombrowski was happy to see him. After all, Smith was his attorney, and it's reasonable to assume he figured Smith had come to get him out. Smith told his client to move over; he was there to join him, not spring him.

Anyone who knew Smith better than merely to nod howdy to might detect a certain cognitive dissonance running around in this narrative. After all, he was a Southern gentleman. He'd learned his law in the company of classmates destined to be the elite of Louisiana's bar at Tulane University. He'd been a prosecutor in the New Orleans district attorney's office. If anyone was to the club, if not precisely the manor, born, it was Ben Smith.

But Smith's estimable pedigree didn't mean he wasn't equal before the law. His arrest was followed by an indictment: for being treasurer and a member of SCEF, and for being a member of the National Lawyers Guild, all in violation of the state's Communist Control Act. Two years later, in its *Dombrowski* decision, the U.S. Supreme Court would throw out the charges and the Communist Control Act along with them.

If Smith wasn't a subversive, he was certainly an oddity. He grew up absorbing traditions and mores that should have been as beyond question as laws of nature. He'd been nurtured and formed, for example, by folkways that consigned African Americans to a permanent condition of second-class dependency. Smith came to find that canon of his culture unacceptable. And yet, his rejection of segregation didn't seem to alienate him in the least from other particularities of his heritage; he remained all his life a thoroughgoing Southerner.

Smith's second wife, Corinne Freeman-Barnwell, thought his break with the single and singular element of his socialization could be traced to his childhood. It was because of a particular experience that, as his wife had it, he "rebelled against his background," a rebellion, it must be emphasized, that was confined to his racial views.

Born in El Dorado, Arkansas, on November 9, 1927, Smith was raised from an early age in the small town of Ruston in upstate Louisiana. It was a region of few paved roads where everyone, farmer or not, lived close to the land. Young Ben was an outdoorsman, tall and broad-chested, comfortable with his physicality. While still a boy, he fished and hunted to put meat on the table of his Methodist household. To prove himself to his exacting father, who placed great value on self-reliance, Ben built a log cabin and performed migrant labor, following the harvest north to Montana. It was while accompanying his father, an officer of a small loan company, to collect loans from black farmers, Freeman-Barnwell believed, that Smith developed his distaste for the systematic oppression of black people. She was certain it was his close contact with poverty-induced misery that turned him against a system that could force so many people to endure the conditions he was routinely exposed to while still a boy.

If the alien sentiment needed validation, an encounter with Henry Wallace when the Progressive Party candidate stopped in Ruston during his 1948 campaign for the presidency supplied it. Wallace's promise to put an end to segregation laws and to open society to the full participation of all citizens, no matter what the color of their skin, struck Smith as an undertaking he'd like to be part of. He joined the Progressive Party and helped it organize on the Tulane campus.

Smith's extensive knowledge of history, mathematics, astronomy, and navigation marks him as a polymath. He put himself through college by enlisting in the Naval Air Corps. The Navy sent him to Rice Institute. He completed his enlistment, then, with the help of the GI Bill, pursued his undergraduate studies at Louisiana Tech and earned a law degree from Tulane.

Smith picked up experience in the New Orleans prosecutor's office and opened his own firm in New Orleans. He hired Marjorie Hamilton, an African American, as his secretary; the sound of the cracking color barrier echoed through the New Orleans central business district. Bruce Waltzer, who later became Smith's law partner, recalls that the management at 234 Loyola Avenue agreed to let Smith employ Hamilton on one condition: she had to wear a custodian's uniform so no one would suspect she wasn't a janitor. Smith promptly found office space elsewhere. Hamilton remained his secretary for many years.

Smith specialized in labor, maritime, and personal injury law and was counsel to the local branch of the maritime union. In his book *The Making of Black Revolutionaries*, Chairman James Forman wrote about the harassing illegal arrests of members of the Student Nonviolent Coordinating Committee doing voter registration work in the South. Smith was all but alone in filing the removal suits required to get the cases into federal courts. "It was a simple procedure," Foreman wrote, "that any lawyer could have carried out if he had had the courage and willingness to openly fight the legal system. . . ." It was Smith's willingness and courage that provoked the authorities into taking action against him.

Smith became increasingly aware in those early days of the movement that what was needed was to lure lawyers down from the North to be surrogates for Southern lawyers who were refusing to become involved. In 1962, he traveled to the National Lawyers Guild's convention in Detroit to join with a few colleagues to make an emotional pitch: you're desperately needed in the South.

The appeal moved the convention to produce the Committee to Assist Southern Lawyers. Smith was named secretary, and the work of the committee soon consumed most of his time and energy. Relief arrived when Kunstler, Stavis, and Kinoy began showing up in his office with sufficient regularity to convince him the cavalry had come to the rescue.

With the National Lawyers Guild under heavy fire for its antiwar work, Smith, in a speech to the guild's 1965 national convention, tried to lift the group's flagging spirits. "We are," he proclaimed, "lawyers in the great tradition of the bar, engaging ourselves in the human history of our era."

It was a remarkable perception at a moment when legal initiatives by the government against all left-wing activism were making a sense of perspective hard to maintain. Still more remarkable is that a man not yet out of his thirties could possess such a keen awareness of the particularity of his own time. He went on to implore his guild comrades to reject despair, shamelessly flaunting a self-defined identification as "a somewhat down-at-the-heels veteran of the courts of the Fifth Circuit."

In one of fate's neater twists, the last law clerk Smith had before he died was Bill Quigley, who in 2009 became the legal director of the Center for Constitutional Rights. By the time Quigley joined him in 1975, Smith was drinking heavily. "He was much more a heart radical than a head radical. Many people thought that's why he abused alcohol, because it just hurt him so much to be involved in so many things, and that was a way of self-medicating." Quigley calls Smith a "brilliant man" and a "visionary."

"'You have to have a chance,' he used to say. 'I don't care if it's one out of a hundred, it's worth fighting and worth doing well.'"

Smith married three times. He had a daughter by his first wife and, with Corinne, his second, adopted two boys and another girl. He died of internal medical problems, the apparent consequence of his drinking, in 1976, at the age of forty-nine.

In his eulogy, James Dombrowski invoked the dark days in the South when blacks who attempted with excessive vigor to register to vote often were thrown in jail. Smith, Dombrowski recalled, was at that time "the only white lawyer in Louisiana or Mississippi who would take a civil rights case."

The Ben Smith Civil Liberties Award is given annually by the Louisiana ACLU. Dombrowski was the recipient of this award in 1981. Bill Quigley received the award in 1986. Bruce Waltzer, Smith's partner, was honored in 1997.

If there are unrecorded but noteworthy events and achievements in Ben Smith's foreshortened life, they are beyond the reach of this account, the result being that Smith remains to a lamentable degree the CCR's lost founder.

CHAPTER 8

Educating

An early *Docket Report* institutionalizes a display of the founders' extravagant presumption. Henceforth, attorneys in search of "both experience in litigation and an atmosphere in which to develop a creative outlook on the use of law as a vehicle for social change" can come to the CCR for instruction. "It is not," the report goes on to affirm, "the purpose of the Center to win abstract legal victories, isolated in an intellectual vacuum from the daily lives of the American people. On the contrary, the Center seeks to make people aware that they *have* rights, and to make those rights a reality." In this way, the Center makes clear that its mission must be understood to include its teaching function. A subsequent report, amplifying the Center's commitment to education, says courtroom victories "are far more meaningful when the underlying issues are understood by the community."

The founders weren't imbued from the beginning with the idea of using their new organization as a teaching tool. That an early name of the group began with the word "Law" isn't insignificant. It was only as they made their way that they encountered the educational possibilities lurking in litigation. The more they saw of those possibilities, the more they were attracted to them.

Education at the CCR takes a variety of forms. At one time, when the office was a more laid-back place, movement activists were welcome to use the facilities for networking, for analyzing their organizational methods, developing strategies. Staff lawyers are expected to find opportunities to write and speak about the work they've done and the lessons they've learned. Many of those lessons find their way into pamphlets. In its case selection process, the Center gives close consideration to an action's potential for reaching out to a broader constituency. "We take cases which have little prospect of success for both the educational and organizational opportunities the cases provide," is the way Arthur Kinoy explained it.

How successfully is the Center's commitment to educate being met?

In 1996 the Center and its co-counsel, Earthright International, brought a case against the Shell Oil company. Shell was charged with complicity in the execution of Nigerian activist Ken Saro Wiwa.

Laura Raymond, of CCR's education and outreach department, says the case was a good fit for the Center. It combined a difficult lawsuit on behalf of worthy clients—Saro Wiwa's relatives—with abundant opportunities for drawing public attention to the ways the oil companies and an accommodating government are despoiling the country.

One such opportunity was a national webcast. Another was a web page. A video got 80,000 hits on YouTube. Law schools were given materials to help them organize events to which participating attorneys journeyed to speak about the case.

Raymond understood her department's mission from the beginning was to use the case to "vitalize the concern and outrage" about continuing human rights abuses and environmental degradation in Nigeria, the issues Saro Wiwa was protesting when he was arrested, convicted, and put to death. In 2009, facing a trial date after thirteen years of throwing up legal obstacles, Shell settled for $15.5 million.

Cases brought against the Blackwater group of military contractors were seen as being rich with possibilities for reaching out to groups concerned about the wars in Iraq and Afghanistan. The Center represented Iraqi plaintiffs hoping to have their day in court against the military contractors they charged had abused them when they were prisoners in Abu Ghraib and other detention centers. "Military contracting is out of control," says a CCR statement. "Contractors far outnumber the U.S military in Afghanistan, making it the most contracted out war in U.S. history." To press its case, the CCR energetically worked to round up support for Stop Outsourcing Security legislation in Congress. Human rights organizations working in Africa increasingly come up against "peacekeepers" working for contractors. Raymond says Blackwater, as an example, has been providing security in certain regions in Darfur. "And that's a really troubling issue that the human rights groups in Africa are very concerned about. We're actually having weekly conference calls with some human rights groups doing work on Africa to talk about this." It's not litigation, it's the CCR as an organizing and teaching mechanism.

When the Center had a Mississippi office, its Beyond the Franchise program graphically illustrated both the educational effort and the result. The staff knew it would be one thing to get disfranchised people into a court of law and come away with a victory. It would be quite another for those same people to learn how to use access to the polls to help them solve problems.

Beyond the Franchise was designed to build on connections the Center's Mississippi staff had cultivated in communities where it fought campaigns and brought court actions to get African Americans registered as voters and onto ballots. Having, for instance, successfully challenged the winner-take-all at-large system in a jurisdiction, Center staffers didn't pack up and move on to the next courthouse. They remained active in the communities to help people understand that casting a ballot is just the beginning of a long, difficult process. It was a graphic example of the way the CCR's legal and educational missions complemented one another.

Margaret Carey, who ran the Center's Greenville office, said it was common for people voting for the first time to think they'd crossed a finish line simply because they'd helped elect a favored candidate. Carey said her job was to convince them they had ongoing responsibilities. It was up to them to make sure their representative delivered on campaign promises.

An example of the way the CCR's legal and teaching functions overlapped: Mississippi wanted to put a hazardous waste facility in Issaquena County. Local people were uncertain. Was it a good thing? Was there anything they could do? Because Carey had recently litigated voting rights cases in the county, "people came to me, black and white. We advised them, and we were prepared to do whatever it was going to take." A referendum was held and the facility was voted down.

In the overwhelmingly black jurisdiction of Tallahatchie County, Mississipi, lawsuits brought by the CCR put African Americans on the county board of supervisors for the first time in the Twentieth Century. Instead of holstering its six-guns and moving on, the Center stayed to help direct energy released by the community's newfound sense of empowerment. Carey described the impact of the electoral victory: "[I]t's almost like it lifted a burden, just a little bit, so that people could see things they didn't see before. In the wake of that victory, you had communities coming together and starting a low-income housing association. They built low-income apartments. They started doing repairs on homes of elderly low-income people. They started construction companies with people in the community to do some of the work." The sizeable stone thus dropped into the county's tranquil swamp of bigotry sent ripples lapping at doors in faraway Washington, where President Bill Clinton's operatives were moved to bestow one of the administration's Enterprise Community designations.

The CCR was by no means responsible for moving the community to a new level of activism. But by maintaining connections, by delivering on the organization's educational component, Carey and her colleagues were in partnership with the community and so played an important role in its transformation.

The Greenville office produced the book-size *Voting Rights: A Manual for Lawyers and Community Activists,* published by the Center in 1986.

Abortion litigation is another arena in which the Center met its determination to instruct. Center attorneys used what they'd learned in pioneering women's movement battles to teach groups such as the Women's Health Collective. "It's an important story," said Rhonda Copelon, "because one of the principles of Center work is you bring real life experiences to the courtroom, and law is part of the organizing process."

Nancy Stearns said what she learned at the Center was not seeing a lawsuit as just a lawsuit but seeing it in a social and political context "as really an organizing device." There was a difference between doing public interest law at the CCR and elsewhere, she said. The difference was the organizing aspect of a CCR case, "the context it got put into. That's something I learned from Arthur, Morty, and Bill."

Copelon located the difference in the way Center attorneys refuse to deal with the law "in terms of law's technicalities, but in terms of law's relationships to the root of the problem."

Stearns expanded on the way a legal action could be shaped so that it would become an educational tool. In the abortion cases, for example, they used not just "the one or two special people that would be the white plaintiffs the way the ACLU would have done it," but instead used three hundred and fifty plaintiffs in New York, a thousand in a New Jersey action, another thousand in Connecticut. It's how the legal action became a way "to get a woman to commit herself to the fight against abortion laws by putting her name there, on the complaint, and by being willing if need be to put her story up front."

Also, as interest generated by court cases brought women out of their homes to find out more, Center lawyers showed up at their meetings and spoke to them about health issues and the legal rights attached to them. With the spread of the astonishing news that women could assert legal rights *as women*, barriers came down. Women began to talk to each other about their difficult experiences with abortion. Some of them, Stearns said, were the women who then went on to become health care advocates for women who continued to need counseling after abortion became legal. It was a striking example of CCR theory that litigation can lead to learning; the newly informed then go on to encourage others to turn to the law for relief.

In 1983, federally funded family planning clinics were required to notify parents when they dispensed contraceptives to the parents' teenage daughters. It became known as the "squeal rule." A CCR lawsuit helped force the government to withdraw the rule. The Center then launched the Squeal Rule Education Project, a public information campaign to get the word to teenagers that it was again safe to ask for family planning advice; their parents wouldn't be told.

A campaign with a strong educational component was the National Jury Project. Along with the National Lawyers Guild, the National Conference of Black Lawyers, the Civil Liberties Defense Fund, and the National Emergency Civil Liberties Committee, the Center founded the Project in 1975. Its purpose was to "counter prejudice in the jury system through jury composition challenges, analyses of jurors' attitudes, screening selection techniques, and legal and educational campaigns to preserve the unanimous jury verdict."

In 1972 Yvonne Wanrow shot and killed a man she said habitually abused her. The state of Washington sentenced her to prison. The CCR represented her in the appeal process and won a reversal. In the wake of *Wanrow*, staff attorney Elizabeth Schneider, cooperating attorney Susan Jordan, and Rutgers law student Cristina Arguedas wrote a paper entitled *Representation of Women Who Defend*

Themselves in Response to Physical or Sexual Assault. Requests for help, from women's groups, from individuals, and from lawyers, poured into the Center. The need for a nationwide source of information on violence against women was clear. The CCR responded in 1978 by creating the Women's Self-Defense Law Project.

The next year, the Center allied itself with educational, religious, legal, community, labor, and civil rights groups to found the National Anti-Klan Network. In keeping with the Network's educational mandate, then executive director Marilyn Clement led a delegation of Center attorneys to Washington to instruct the House Judiciary Subcommittee on Criminal Justice on means the federal government has at its disposal to monitor and regulate Klan activities.

Education was the goal in the mid-1980s when the CCR joined with other organizations in arraigning the United States before war crimes tribunals. "The tribunals on U.S. responsibility for crimes in Central America and the Caribbean," the 1985–86 Docket Report states, "helped to make people aware of this nation's illegal and inhumane actions in those areas."

Some victims of repression and of wars in the region made their way north. The government rounded them up and sent them back. A handful of churches and synagogues offered them sanctuary. The government insisted no right of sanctuary inhered in houses of worship, an assertion the Center contested in court without success. Nevertheless, responding to the legal questions raised by the sanctuary movement, it published a pamphlet, *Havens of Refuge,* that immediately became a widely used tool in the struggles to keep the refugees safe. Again, the legal is midwife to the educational.

In 1987 the Center organized a meeting in Washington of AIDS workers, lawyers, and other health care activists around the issue of AIDS and women's reproductive rights, then went on to launch a national campaign to focus attention on the problem.

In the same year, 1987, the Center played a key role in organizing the campaign that blocked Robert Bork's confirmation for a seat on the Supreme Court.

A spottier educational record has been compiled in lawyer training. Ironically, the most specific teaching function the founders had in mind when they included education in their plans was training lawyers in movement law. Under the press of heavy caseloads, however, it was easy for each of the four to neglect mentoring duties.

Morton Stavis was convinced no staff attorney should stay much longer than three years, four at the outside. They should learn the ropes and move on. Former legal director Frank Deale thought that's not enough time to train lawyers adequately. He pointed out that the average length of a Center case that goes to trial is six years. Deale thought young attorneys should be encouraged to stay at least that long at the Center. He said, "You can't really consider yourself an experienced lawyer until you've taken a case from start to finish."

Some early staffers believed salaries were kept low and workloads heavy partly to discourage long tenures. "What I could easily do and happily do and not feel I was sacrificing at all at twenty-five or even thirty," said Nancy Stearns, "begins to feel like a sacrifice at forty. It was a setup that really was only possible for very young lawyers or lawyers who were financially independent. So it did seem to me that what the Center was trying to do was get rid of people as they got older, and just have it as a training thing with the old guys as voluntary staff attorneys and all young people, and I wasn't sure that was a good thing to do."

Training, former legal director Michael Deutsch explains, is ideally the province of the legal director. Prior to Deutsch, however, the two times the title had been bestowed it was on a senior attorney who didn't want the job and who taught, if at all, by example rather than instruction. Even though he wasn't on hand, Deutsch believes the political climate in the early years ensured that young attorneys arrived with a sense of commitment already firmly in place. Combine that commitment with the frenzy of activity that characterized life at the Center, and new arrivals were schooled by the sink-or-swim system of pedagogy. Times change. Deutsch says lawyers subsequently coming on board hadn't learned the law "in the crucible of the movement." They were usually in their early thirties. They had had some experience, seldom much in trial work. Getting them up to speed was one of the tasks Deutsch was charged with when he was hired in 1993. "They really wanted me to come in and start a mentoring program and also call on the resources of some of our more experienced voluntary and cooperating attorneys. . . . There's this idea that being a courtroom lawyer, you have to get to a certain level, a wall, and unless you get over that wall you're always shy about doing it." It was his job, and by extension the Center's, to build new recruits' experience sufficiently to get them over the wall. It was an obligation honored mostly in the breach.

A contributing reason for neglecting the training function was that for many years the staff resisted having a legal director, preferring instead to make collective decisions on new cases and to allot responsibility for cases on the basis of enthusiasm rather than assignment. Staff attorneys understood they were supposed to help new arrivals develop skills, but they weren't in the habit of thinking of themselves as trainers. Mostly, they tried to discharge their duty informally, by being available to talk about what they were up to at any given time. "We always discussed what we were going to do," said Rhonda Copelon. "We circulated our briefs. In the collective process, we trained new arrivals. But we never institutionalized that, and that was a problem." Still, she remembered the CCR's impact on her own development fondly. "I felt like I was expected, in the positive sense, to be a great lawyer. I loved the fact that I was in an institution that had confidence in me."

Deutsch contends that for a period there was a singular exception to the training nonfeasance. "Everybody says that if there was one mentor here it was Mort Stavis. He really did in fact train a lot of lawyers to be civil rights lawyers."

Whatever the level of mentoring, its reception by new hires grew more problematic with the shifting political climate. It was a time when the New Left was consigning much of the Old Left's politics to the dustbin. After the ferment that informed the 1970s, attorneys arriving at the Center were more evolved in their political development. Rather than accept anyone at random, Stavis included, as mentors, they wanted to be sure their closely calibrated ideas about what was and wasn't politically acceptable were applied to their training. It was a formula for tension. And often a deterrent to teaching.

The Center has a better record for instructing lawyers who aren't members of its staff. It systematically passes along to any and all interested attorneys lessons it learns in the course of litigation. It employs a variety of means. One is simply to engage in informal exchanges with like-minded attorneys around the country. Litigators embarking on cases with constitutional implications, as, so outstandingly, in Guantánamo cases, contact Center lawyers for a crash course in strategy and tactics. Experience is shared, too, by providing research assistance to lawyers and movements embarked on litigation in a familiar field.

Center attorneys have given expert testimony to committees of Congress and the United Nations. They've served as consultants to such official bodies as the U.S. Office of Economic Opportunity.

Still another means of getting out the CCR message is through law schools. Many staff attorneys leave active duty at the Center to teach. The lessons they learned at the CCR are passed along to their students. Most of these alumni retain their connection to the Center, some by signing on to be voluntary staff attorneys. Others maintain the looser relationship of cooperating attorney. Staff attorneys often are invited by law schools to deliver guest lectures.

Many law firms use interns for cheap labor, while the partners take credit for making a contribution to the profession in the form of lawyer training. Dorothy Zellner saw a way to elevate the use of interns to a more formal, more productive program. She organized the Ella Baker Student Project in the spring of 1987. To make the program attractive to top-level students, the Ella Baker project offers more than mere exposure to a law office. It includes a curriculum of films about movements for social change. Seminars are conducted by scholars, activists, and clients. Subjects vary, but over the years they've included the history of the civil rights movement, public interest law, international law, government misconduct, racial justice, lesbian and gay rights, women's rights, and reproductive rights litigation.

From the hundreds of applications that come in to the project each year, between ten and thirteen are selected. Zellner says that when she was interviewing applicants they were overwhelmingly female. Aware that the CCR's constituency, its client base, was preponderantly people of color and women and lesbians and gays, Zellner reached out to those groups to see to it they were represented among the interns. "Basically, what we wanted was to develop movement lawyers. They were looking for experience in constitutional law, and we wanted people who showed some indication that they were willing to take this experience and turn it into a lifelong commitment." Summer interns work five days a week for ten weeks.

The rest of the year, the Center makes use of two or three students at a time from law schools in the New York area. Over the course of a year, some twenty students gain direct exposure to the work of the CCR. All applicants, whether or not they were ultimately selected for the Ella Baker program, become members of a talent pool from which future staff attorneys can be recruited. Current executive director Vincent Warren was an Ella Baker intern.

Finally, the CCR meets its commitment to education through its publications program. An elaborate Annual Report has replaced the old docket reports. It describes new cases and the status of cases previously chronicled. These descriptions are also available on the Center's website (ccrjustice.com).

A quarterly newsletter is issued. Other publications are softcover books, pamphlets, occasional position papers on major Center campaigns, and a sporadically appearing newspaper, *CCR News*. Together with the National Lawyers Guild, the Center, as noted above, published a still-valued manual on how to represent witnesses appearing before federal grand juries. The Center pamphlet *If an Agent Knocks, Federal Investigations and Your Rights* has lost its subtitle and been brought up to date to include e-mail and cell phone monitoring along with broad-scale advice on electronic security. It remains after some thirty years the definitive resource on the subject.

CHAPTER 9

Strike!

In May of 1994, co-president Arthur Kinoy spoke about what was being done at the CCR to address internal tensions. He recognized that a staff/board structure comes with built-in conflicts and contradictions. The Center, he was sure, was nonetheless solving its problems.

Why was he sure? Because of his conviction that "the people" would not be confounded, would ineluctably, irresistibly get it right. "The board is made up of people involved in people's movements all over the country." Kinoy hadn't the least doubt that staff and board were inseparably bound by their goal to work on behalf of those movements. Five months later the entire staff struck. Walked out. The magazine *The Progressive* said the strike "threatened to tear apart a major progressive institution."

The conflicts and contradictions Kinoy spoke about had their roots in the staff collective that formed by default in the organization's early years. Being attorneys, the founders knew about legal and fiscal responsibility and duly equipped their new organization with a board of directors. What they failed to do was define the board's authority. For years there was no administrative staff. Money was short, and they could manage the office themselves. Besides, the cases the Center was litigating were *their* cases. Any decisions that had to be made, *they* would make. Their assumption from the beginning was that they would run the CCR, while the board provided legal cover and helped raise money for salaries and overhead and travel expenses.

Kinoy recalled a time when the firm of Kunstler, Kunstler, and Kinoy and the Law Center for Constitutional Rights barely had separate identities. "In those days we [KK& K] were working inside of the Center. When someone came to us, and Bill and I would think, 'This is something the Center should be handling,' we would say to the people there, 'Here's a Center case.'"

It was growth, of course, that turned this simple, smooth-running machine into a clunker. Work increasing at a rate the founders couldn't keep up with meant adding people to the staff. Memories become clouded, but there is general agreement that these new lawyers and legal workers, because they were on the scene when decisions had to be made, began making them. Staff lawyers, inevitably, had begun generating their own cases.

Furthermore, the seniors weren't always around. Kunstler, for instance, was away for long periods, at first in the South and later in connection with the Chicago Seven case. With the CCR resettled in New York City and his teaching duties confining him much of the time to New Jersey, Kinoy was often unavailable. Smith was based in New

Orleans. Weiss was at the office more or less regularly after 1969, but he had all the executive responsibilities he wanted at his law firm. Only Stavis shouldered the burden of providing leadership, but even he had teaching duties and a private practice to attend to and a home and family in Newark.

As a consequence of this general leadership vacuum, the CCR staff, when it worked on cases not under the direct supervision of the seniors, was left increasingly to its own devices. Kunstler's interpretation of the fallout was characteristically blunt. He charged the board with making "a terrible mistake" by, through its inaction, permitting the staff to "degenerate into a collective." To begin, the board had little experience with hands-on management of the organization. Members traditionally were content to limit their function to hiring the executive director, providing the organization with its required legal cover, and furnishing overall political direction. Moreover, Kunstler's judgment seems as insensitive to what was going on in that special world in which the Center operated as it is harsh.

The New Left was ascendant. Kinoy's "people" were everywhere being demoted, replaced by individuals "doing their own thing." New staff members at the Center often reflected this fragmented radical politics.

When she was a staff attorney in the 1970s, Elizabeth Schneider says, she and her colleagues were accustomed to a large degree of autonomy and very little oversight. "We went back and forth for years on the pros and cons of having a legal director to report to."

The staff at the time was small, six or seven. Its members introduced a modicum of system. The guidelines about how a case could be brought were understood in an informal way. If the case seemed to raise important issues, it almost certainly found a home. The same was true if it assisted a group that was underrepresented in the better funded, better organized world. "And frequently," says Schneider, "it came down to, did somebody really want to do it. Or, even if we didn't have the people power, did we really think it was something important to do. Those issues would get hashed out." Staff meetings were every other Monday afternoon. Anyone, lawyer or legal worker, could present a case. Good will and a sense of responsibility to a common cause ensured that decisions were made.

How Center people felt about how well the organization functioned under the guidance of a staff collective depends often but not always on which side of the board–staff dichotomy they belonged. Staff attorney Matthew Chachere represented his colleagues in negotiations with the board during the '94 crisis. When the staff struck and joined an affiliate of the United Auto Workers, he was named shop steward. The CCR's 1994 entry-level salary of $29,000 for attorneys was, said Chachere, the lowest of any public interest law office in the New York area. "People were willing to put in the hours and to work for the pay because it was ours." Chachere positioned the collective at the center of the CCR's success not only in litigation but in fundraising as well. Because, he said, they saw an extraordinary commitment on the part of the CCR staff, funders recognized that they would get "a tremendous bang for their buck in giving to the Center."

Dorothy Zellner speaks about the way the CCR functioned before the strike and its subsequent reorganization: "[The CCR] wasn't the most efficient of offices if you're using the standard of AT&T. There was a lot of time spent with people sitting and talking. But what made people come

[t]here, especially lawyers who worked at an abominable rate of pay compared to almost anywhere else, was that they had real, serious input, not only into the kind of cases they would take, but into the whole life of the organization."

Some, though, were aware of deep systemic flaws. The collective, in the opinion of Nancy Stearns, "wasn't real." She says it refused to take on unpleasant administrative burdens and cites her sense of being exploited, not by the board but by the staff, as one of the reasons she left the Center. There came a time, she says, when she could no longer work "someplace where everybody got paid the same and there were vast disparities in the amount everybody worked." No one wanted to call the slackers to account. "It's hard to confront people," says Stearns. "As a result, you did a disservice to the person who really needed to be criticized or maybe really needed to be moved out because they weren't functioning. We were never able to do it."

Longtime executive director Marilyn Clement, in a 1988 report to the board, pointed to a paradox in the way the collective functioned. The collective, she argued, encouraged individualism and so *made it impossible to work collectively* [original emphasis]." With no one able to tell anyone what to do, each person on staff was relatively free to work independently of everyone else. Clement's report said there were occasions "when the staff 'collective' told the lawyers that we wanted to do a certain case or that we wanted to increase our docket in a certain area, but no lawyer was interested in doing it—therefore it didn't get done." Her report characterized the way the Center operated as "basically anarchical."

Michael Ratner says the collective routinely approved cases brought in by its members. "It was, 'we'll help you if you'll help us,' so everybody's off litigating in their own little corners, rather than a core of people trying to really push something." Because the CCR was a small institution with a small budget, he says, it follows that "you don't make much progress unless you are together."

Frank Deale, meanwhile, has only praise for the staff's commitment to consensual decision-making. Having said that, he tells of a time when collectivity led the group astray: In the process of hiring a lawyer, the votes of the majority of staff lawyers were overridden by the legal workers' votes. "That, to me," says Deale, "was collectivity gone mad."

"For all the years I was there," says David Cole, referring to his tenure as a staff attorney, "there was a consistent theme: on the one hand we love our freedom and our autonomy and our ability to respond to new cases because we don't have rigid responsibilities. On the other hand, what do you do when things aren't working? Who takes responsibility?" He says when someone did step up and try to call attention to a problem area, the staff would gather its forces and attack back and make that person regret having acted responsibly.

When asked if he could point out weaknesses in the structure prior to the 1994 crisis, William Kunstler said the staff had been allowed to accumulate too much power and had become "almost dictatorial" in the way the Center operated. He cited as an example the collective's refusal to let lawyers run drug cases through the Center, even when such cases came with a political component congruent with the Center's ideology.

And yet, despite its haphazard structure, its failure to provide clear and consistent leadership and its prickly relations with the board, the collective ran the CCR for nearly two decades. The collectivists' sense of controlling their own destinies clearly inspired many if not all to extend themselves beyond customary limits in their commitment to their work. They were where they wanted to be, doing work they fervently believed in, for all practical purposes under the direction of no authority. What could be more rewarding?

Dr. Vicki Alexander, regarded by many of the Center's staff as a "little Stalin" for unremittingly insisting on the board's prerogatives, acknowledged the collective's contribution to the accomplishments of the early years. She says it was impossible to deny that the staff managed to operate effectively without leadership or a solid structure. She attributes the change from a collective that functioned to one that didn't in part to the impact the collapse of the Soviet Union had on movement politics in the United States.

The CCR, a deeply embedded cohort of movement politics, could scarcely have emerged unscathed from the turmoil of the period. For one, instead of being movement-driven, new recruits arrived with worthy but disparate agendas. The more anti-sexist you could be, the more anti-racist you could be, the "more pure" you were, says Alexander. As, increasingly, new staffers were selected for their political "purity," the collective ceased to be inspired by whatever defining impulse once lent it a degree of cohesion. To come into the 1990s looking for a position citing your devotion to "the movement" would have stamped you as quaint if not slightly ridiculous. Hiring at the Center, Alexander says, "became affirmative action to the max." In short, the New Left had come to the CCR.

Whatever bonds held the staff together for the organization's first twenty years began to loosen. Morton Stavis's widow, Esther, remembered watching it happen. The time came, she recalled, when incoming lawyers declined to conform to established patterns and ways of thinking. "Some of them wanted to go off in all directions. Somebody had to hold the place together, and that was what Morty tried to do. Toward the end, it seemed to be what he was doing full-time—trying to keep these young people from going off in all directions."

Ratner offers a theory consistent with Alexander's. "Part of it was the changing political times . . . there was less cohesive politics and it became harder to get people to work together on things. Another difference may have had to do with racial and class politics. Maybe without an over-guiding politics to it, that stuff came to the surface more." He doubts that a decline in the quality of the recruits contributed to the change, pointing out that Center people moved on to have successful careers. "So you'd have to say there was something endemic about the working conditions that brought out the worst in people" during that period.

It was the period, then, the intensity and peculiarity of it, that had taken a grip on left politics. Ratner continues: "Something happened in the leadership, something happened in the politics . . ." He leaves it unfinished. It isn't a thing that can be readily explained.

Beth Stephens believes that as staff and board raced toward a climactic collision, the only way to head it off would have been to incorporate the board into the collective. The conflict was otherwise irreconcilable, because full-time staff members had come to feel that they had "a piece of the ownership of the place," while board members felt left out and disrespected because of decisions made in their absence and without their input. Equally, staff members, according to Stephens, were resentful of decisions taken by board members who weren't "contributing to the day-to-day work."

An attempt to bring staff and board into a more productive working alliance was made in response to the fiscal crisis of 1992, When the board determined that layoffs had to be made, it met over a weekend with the staff. A new organizational structure was to be hammered out. Under the new structure there was an executive committee responsible to the board. Joint committees included a finance committee, a personnel committee, and a development committee. The personnel committee was assigned the task of writing a personnel manual, which, among other things, set out clear hiring and firing procedures. Key decisions were henceforth to be made only after staff and board had a chance to respond to the other's position, with the appropriate joint committee serving as mediator.

Referring to the personnel manual that she helped draft, Stephens says she thought it resolved some of the persistent concerns about supervision and discipline. She believes it created a structure that could have worked had it been implemented.

As part of the restructuring, Ratner was named the CCR's first legal director. He says when he tried to discharge his duties as defined in the new manual, "I got killed." He recalls trying to discipline someone who, records proved, hadn't come to work thirty days out of sixty. The manual gave the accused a right to appeal to the collective. The staff, says Ratner, called his disciplinary action "a racist decision."

Two things are clear: one is that where implementation of the new structure was attempted it didn't work; the other is that the structure's failure brought about the collective's ultimate destruction. Blame for the failure resides in part with the staff's refusal to work with Clement's successor as executive director, Miriam Thompson.

A policy adopted by the management team in 1986 subjected new staffers to evaluation by their supervisors after six months of their employment and again after their first year. The '92 crisis triggered a broad consensus that many Center problems were traceable to the breakdown of this evaluation process. New procedures were laboriously drawn up and adopted, and Thompson tried to activate them. "We tried to save Miriam," says Alexander. "The staff wouldn't talk to her. So finally she was forced to resign." Clement charges that the staff "drove Miriam out because she was moving on evaluations."

With Thompson gone, the staff was once again without direction. The evaluation procedures enshrined in the new personnel manual were left untested. Without accountability, some on staff were less than zealous in their devotion to their work. Productivity and fund-raising dropped off.

Evaluation of lawyers was the specified responsibility of the executive director, taking leads from the legal director, a member of the directorate. Frank Deale had reluctantly succeeded Ratner. He had little inclination to start passing judgment on his colleagues and so resigned to go into teaching. The board put forward the name of Michael Deutsch to replace Deale. Deutsch had years of experience in movement law in the Chicago area. Clement says the staff resisted. "They wanted to put in somebody who was very weak . . . [and] they knew Michael was going to come in knowing what he was doing and in a position to evaluate what everybody else was doing." Alexander says the board's unanimous support of Deutsch's candidacy left little room for the staff to assert its right of appointment.

The board made certain Deutsch understood that the job description included an obligation to make staff evaluations. Nonetheless, according to Stephens, Deutsch "said he wanted to wait until Ron [Daniels] had started full-time as the new executive director [later in the year, 1994], because he wanted that kind of backup. And then he just didn't do it." Once again, instead of pressing the issue, the board let it slide.

In September 1994, the board gave the staff its response to the latest financial crisis: two staff positions would be eliminated, one white attorney and one white legal worker. Daniels and Deutsch were asked to accept ten percent salary cuts, and staff members were given twenty percent cuts plus a one-month furlough. Ratner suggests some board members may have thought it expedient to fire white staffers rather than people of color. The final, ill-fated decision on the two terminations included an African-American legal worker. The staff rallied around their pink-slipped comrades. There were, of course, no written evaluations. Without written evaluations to support the board's contention that it was firing people who weren't productive, Ratner calls the decisions on which staff people were to be let go arbitrary. "I said, 'how can you do this? Is there anything in their files, a piece of paper that says they're not doing the job?' "

Zellner thinks the tough terms were part of a plot to get rid of the collective once and for all. She says, instead of invoking the crisis management procedures put in place in 1992, the board seized its opportunity to declare the collective unworkable. "So," says Zellner, "that was the issue of power."

Ratner agrees power was the issue. "I think when the crisis started, it wasn't the intention to end the collective. I think the issue was giving the executive committee the authority to make the layoffs they thought were necessary." He says most board members, including himself, agreed the operation of the Center needed to be fundamentally changed. "The majority of people said two things. They said, 'I don't want to run this place.' And the second thing they said was, 'We're fed up.'" And so they acquiesced to letting colleagues who *were* willing to "run the place" develop an attack, ostensibly on the organization's financial problems and possibly on the collective as well.

Alexander's criticisms of the organization's performance began in July of '94, well before the extent of the money crisis was fully known. She partly blamed declining vigor and productivity on the leadership vacuum in the wake of Thompson's resignation nearly two years earlier, but she attributed poor performance mostly to "a very weak structure" that had permitted the Center to take on new lawyers who didn't meet the organization's standards. Collective decision-making, she charged, contaminated the hiring process. "It's very time consuming, and also sometimes the concerns with race, class, sex, and so on can become barriers to really moving forward."

The staff continued to resist the notion of pay raises based on length of service: unequal salaries would lead to a class structure. A consequence of keeping salaries close to parity was that experienced lawyers didn't apply. Alexander asserted in July that the Center's hiring procedures were "something we need to transform to get us out of this morass."

Peter Weiss also connects the salary issue to the transformation he believed the collective underwent in the 1980s from a mechanism that functioned to one that foundered. As they accumulated seniority, some asked to be paid on a scale more consistent with their years of service and increased responsibilities. "Basically," says Weiss, "it was the junior people who forced out the senior people on the old principle of parity." Weiss denies the board set out from the beginning to dismantle the collective. Instead, he contends it is significant that the 1994 docket in no way met the period's political imperatives. The board, he says, "had a better sense of where the Center ought to be moving," but was being held back by the staff "from responding to the needs of the times." None of that, he adds, was seen very clearly by the board when the process of dealing with the growing '94 crisis began. It emerged clearly, he says, only when the staff "decided it wouldn't accept leadership from the board."

In May 1994, Ron Daniels had been executive director of the CCR for less than a month. He learns the group's way of conducting business, how the staff presides over the hiring of the legal director to whom it theoretically reports, how new cases must be voted on by all staff members including receptionists. "If there's much more democracy inside CCR than in most organizations, it means that you're not, as an executive director, the chief executive officer with the final say on things. Your role is to lead, but it's leading by participation and involvement and using skills and experience to bring the collective to consensus." He sees his challenge as finding ways to win the goodwill of the collective and to mediate between board and staff "to get the outcome you need." He doesn't know it at the time, but he has only four months to consolidate his power with the collective.

Years later, looking back, he pronounces the process "intriguing." More than a little ruefully, he says there was "a politics to the power of the position."

By September 1994, the CCR was forced to confront yet another round of damaging income shortfalls and busted budgets. Some members of the board saw the new financial crunch as providing an opening for a showdown on the issue of where in the organization authority ultimately resided. This time, they had Ron Daniels riding shotgun.

He'd arrived arrayed in more, and more adroit, executive experience than anyone before him. As an African American with a long and gaudy record of activism, he'd be a tough target. Deale says that as the crisis approached, Daniels had to decide whether he was going to work with the staff or work with the board. "I think it really came to that stark a choice. He had to go one way or the other. He went with the board, and he lost the staff."

According to Daniels, he pushed the board into taking a hard line. He says a decision had to be made about reducing the size of the staff. "The board had always kicked that decision to the staff. . . . I insisted that the board take its fiduciary responsibility." He points out that legally, in a corporation, the board is in charge, and staffs have no authority. But when the CCR board bypassed the staff and ordered two people fired, "it was utter chaos." Daniels says a member of the staff shouted at him, "You tell the board to get down here!" He adds that the staff was quite prepared to discipline the board. Among those who were let go was Audrey Seniors, a black legal worker whose tenure at the CCR was long and who, moreover, was in poor health. A strike vote was taken. Every member of the staff except Margaret Carey in the Greenville office walked out.

Daniels's glittering credentials provided no shelter from the storm: he was labeled a racist. "I took big hits. I was ostracized in the African-American community. There were actually people who circulated a letter calling me all kinds of names. It was very, very brutal."

"They became totally vicious," Kunstler recalled about the staff. "They said we were all mean sons of bitches." Deale, even though he was no longer on staff, voiced strong opposition to "the people who have taken control" and filed an affidavit with the National Labor Relations Board in support of the strikers. Board member Patricia Williams resigned in protest (she later returned), condemning both sides as "a classic case of the left devouring itself." "Even with the goal of ending the collective," Stephens says, the board "horribly mishandled it."

For seven weeks, people came by to observe the spectacle of a picket line outside the CCR's office building.

The strike was settled on purely economic terms. Returning staff would be paid their full salaries. A severance package was part of the settlement. All but five of the staff accepted the package and promptly resigned. The rest stayed on only briefly. The collective was no more. The organization soldiered on with Deutsch and cooperating attorneys bearing most of the burden.

Daniels calls the period immediately following the strike "the reshaping." It was a process, he says, of working with the few remaining staff "to begin to get a structure that could hopefully preserve the best of the collective, the best of the collaboration, but still allow . . . the management, to make decisions and to be able to move the organization." He acknowledges that the problem was finding a balance between a corporatist model, with all decisions coming down from above, and the collective formation that was being replaced. "It wasn't easy. There was a dynamic tension."

Deutsch says people who mourn the passing of the way the collective was in its heyday overlook the difficulties. He insists the process was continually a source of problems.

Ratner says that in the final years of its existence, the collective had been making it possible for people to be on staff and do nothing. "There was no work being done. I couldn't have raised a nickel for that place the last three years. They did it with mirrors. It was a fraud, taking money from people at the end. I consider it that bad." Rhonda Copelon said the collective "outlived its time."

The search for a more perfect marriage of board and staff continues to this day. It's what executive director Vincent Warren calls the organization's "perennial struggle." The staff, he says, has to have input, but what type and how much are subjects of continuous debate. Clearly, there is no ideal formula for meeting the occasionally conflicting demands of the managers and those they manage. That the CCR refuses to give up the search speaks either to its principles or to its native attachment to the long shot.

Kinoy's perspective was a long and characteristically confident one. Board–staff tensions at the CCR, he said, were no worse than those experienced "by every organization doing any kind of positive work . . . you always have these problems."

Speaking in the aftermath of the strike, Weiss put the matter in dialectical terms: "The collective thesis has outlived its usefulness. The current somewhat centralized managerial antithesis will do okay for awhile. After that, I think we're going to move into a new synthesis, where there will again be genuine cooperation between the staff and the board and where there will be consultation for the purpose of action and not for the purpose of frustrating action, which was often the case in the past."

Daniels was clearly more at home with the new "somewhat centralized managerial antithesis" than he was when he was confronted with the challenge of winning the collective's goodwill. As a result, he says when speaking of a "paradigm shift in terms of authority," the management team was able to make final decisions and be held accountable by the board. However, he denies that the new structure was top-down in any traditional sense. He says it was "hierarchical theoretically, but in practice it was more collaborative and more cooperative." The goal of the new paradigm, he insists, was "to maintain the best of the collective and do away with the part that seemed to be dysfunctional."

Weiss has no doubt that "we very much needed an executive director with Ron's politics." Ratner agrees. Having someone with a political rather than a legal background in charge of Center operations is "a strong thing in that it makes sure the law is involved in political movements."

Until the death of the collective, the theory was that the executive director kept the collective plugged into the movement, while the collective grounded the executive director's politics in jurisprudential reality. That grounding, since the passing of the collective, has been the responsibility of the legal director. In Vincent Warren, the Center believes it has a deeply politicized executive director who has the added advantage of having been trained in the law.

If Kinoy was right that the internal political issues at the Center were similar to those that other movement organizations were experiencing at the time, there is no question that the 1994 strike by the staff set the Center's problems apart in terms of their impact. That the organization survived the crisis was testimony to the commitment of Center people to the work they were doing, to work still to be done, and to the work done by those who were there before them.

CHAPTER 10

Getting Down to Cases

The cases summarized here hardly make up an exhaustive narrative of what the Center's been up to over the course of its short life. Not all are seminal. Nor even especially representative. They have been chosen with an eye to their impact. In a few instances, the impact was on the law. Or it was on the national zeitgeist. Most often, it was on the Center and its staff. Some of the cases occupied positions on the organization's docket for so many years they threatened to become a way of life for the staff members who were shepherding them through the system. Some demanded a degree of dedication so beyond customary responsibilities that they took a heavy toll.

INTERNATIONAL HUMAN RIGHTS AND SOLIDARITY

Filártiga v. Peña-Iral

The Center exhibited little more than characteristic audacity in 1969 when it tried to bring a suit against the United States government for the destruction of the village of My Lai in Vietnam. The action was dropped when the government of North Vietnam declined to become involved. Preparation for the suit, however, had uncovered 28 U.S.C. 1350.

The Alien Tort Claims Act is, or was, an obscure law passed in 1789. Under the act, an alien has a right to bring suit in a federal court for a tort, or civil claim. The accused must be available, which is to say within the jurisdiction of the court. In the eighteenth century, the law that would be applied to such a suit was called the law of nations, now known as international law.

Ten years pass. Peter Weiss gets a call from Amnesty International. A Paraguayan man is being held for deportation in the Brooklyn Navy Yard. When he was a police chief in Paraguay, he tortured to death the seventeen-year-old son of Dr. Joel Filártiga. Filártiga, an outspoken opponent of Paraguayan dictator Alfredo Stroessner, wants to sue the cop. Can Weiss stop the deportation and get him into court? "We convened an emergency session at the Center," Weiss remembers. "Somebody said, 'That's the Alien Tort Claims Act, the one we dug up for My Lai.'" They discover the victim's sister Dolly is in New York; she'll be the plaintiff.

Some people in the room are less than thrilled about their chances of getting into a U.S. court a case involving a Paraguayan citizen against another Paraguayan citizen dealing with acts that took place in Paraguay. "Our position," Weiss remembers, "was all you had to have was the physical presence of the defendant in the jurisdiction of the American court to go forward with a case like that, a position that was ultimately vindicated."

Within twenty-four hours, the CCR team, led by Weiss and Rhonda Copelon, draws up papers and goes into the Eastern District Court in Brooklyn. They file their suit and obtain an injunction to prevent the defendant's deportation.

The district court judge later voided his own injunction. The policeman, Peña-Irala, was about to slip out of the Center's grasp. A swift appeal briefed the court on the emergence since the Nuremberg trials after the Second World War of an international law of human rights. It argued that present-day torturers are, or should be in the eyes of the law, no different than eighteenth-century pirates who were declared for legal purposes *hostes humani generis*—enemies of all humanity.

The suit ended in a default judgment in favor of Dolly Filártiga for $10.4 million. But more important, it extended the reach of U.S. courts. It established the principle that those who commit serious human rights violations in another country and then enter the United States may be sued by their victims in federal court. *Filártiga* became the CCR's most widely recognized landmark case.

Not everyone is equally enthusiastic about the way *Filártiga* opened the way for the federal judiciary to involve itself in the internal affairs of other countries. Attorney Victor Rabinowitz told me that he argued with Arthur Kinoy when *Filártiga* was brought. With his partners Leonard Boudin and Michael Standard, Rabinowitz represented the interests of the Cuban government in the United

States. "I said that if a U.S. court can snatch a citizen from Paraguay and hold him responsible for a crime committed in Paraguay, then they could do exactly the same thing to a representative of Cuba." In 1963, in *Banco Nacional de Cuba v. Sabatino,* the Rabinowitz firm had based its case on the "act of state doctrine." It holds that what a state does within its own borders is its own business. Courts of other countries have no right to interfere. "The Center people scoff at it," said Rabinowitz, "but it's still my Bible. We won eight to one in the Supreme Court. *Filártiga* was a terrible violation of that principle."

Rabinowitz doubted that anyone knows what international law really means. There are, he said, many theories. "There's the theory of natural law—peace and justice and so on. Then there's the school that says what countries have always done—the customs and practices of nations—is international law. The slave trade was justified under this doctrine."

In his 1996 memoir, *Unrepentant Leftist,* Rabinowitz holds that most lawyers agree that international law is "a pretentious fraud, a legal fiction which enables governments to act in accordance with their national interests while preaching sanctimoniously about a 'law' which does not exist." And so, he argues, the attempt by legal scholars to define international law becomes "an essay in philosophy rather than an essay in jurisprudence."

Apart from definition, the problem is one of enforcement. For instance, Rabinowitz had little use for the growing practice of declaring people war criminals. He saw the question of who is and who isn't a war criminal as depending not so much on law as on who wins the war. He offered Bosnia as a case in point.

Former executive editor of *The New York Times* Max Frankel took up the same theme in a *New York Times Magazine* article. He deplored the "pretense" that world leaders are willing to subject themselves to the constrictions of some universally recognized system of laws. "The ugly truth is that international crime pays. Aggressors walk free if they win the wars they start. Atrocities are customarily cited only against losers."

Estate of Himoud Saed Abtan, et al. v. Prince, et al.

This case graphically demonstrates the way *Filártiga* continues to provide a tool for aggressive litigation.

In September of 2007, a convoy of vehicles operated by the U.S. security company then known as Blackwater drove into Baghdad's Nisour Square. Later claiming to believe they felt threatened, a number of Blackwater's men opened fire on civilians in the square, killing seventeen and wounding at least twenty.

Later the same year the Center and independent counsel Susan Burke represented several family members of victims of the shooting in Nisour Square in a suit brought against Erik Prince, Blackwater's president, and against his firm's affiliated companies. Charges under the Alien Tort Statute (ATS) included war crimes and summary executions. An earlier Center case, *Doe v. Karadžić* (1993, see below), was cited as precedent for the relevance of ATS. The charges further stated that Blackwater "created and fostered a culture of lawlessness among its employees, encouraging them to act in the company's financial interest at the expense of innocent human life," in the process violating a variety of international, federal, and state laws. The defendants claimed that because their employees in Iraq were under contract to the military, they were immune from liability. If a civil action could be brought, they argued, it should be not against them but against the government of the United States. Not unaware of a nice irony, CCR attorneys joined with their counterparts in the Department of Justice in beating back this effort.

Blackwater had changed its name to Xe by the time it settled for an undisclosed sum in January 2010. Katherine Gallagher, in the final period the Center's lead attorney on the case, says it's the only case in which "foreign victims received compensation from a military contractor." She says the plaintiffs are well aware that a good and sufficient reason for Blackwater to change its name is because of image problems it encountered, both in the United States and throughout the world, after Nisour Square. "I think that gives some feeling of achievement."

Republic of the Philippines v. Ferdinand E. Marcos, et al.

Three days after dictator Ferdinand Marcos fled his country on February 25, 1986, the new Philippine government retained counsel in the United States. It asked the CCR to recover millions of dollars' worth of property along with other assets the Marcos regime had stolen from the Philippine people that were being held in the United States. No one knew how much money was at stake. Some estimates put the total amount illegally transferred out of the country by Marcos as exceeding the $30 billion Philippine national debt. Recovering as much as possible of this treasure was vital to the battered Philippine economy.

Time was a factor. Dummy corporations owned by Marcos held four valuable commercial buildings in New York City and a large estate in Nassau County on Long Island. If the properties could be quickly liquidated, the proceeds of the sales could be hidden.

Morton Stavis took the lead role. Volunteer attorney Mahlon Perkins remembers that he, Stavis, and another volunteer, Ralph Shapiro, began work over a weekend to be ready to block any sales when the new week began. Three days after accepting the case, the Center had a court-ordered freeze on the New York properties. Further, it enlisted cooperating attorneys around the country to locate other Marcos assets.

The defendants removed the New York case to the federal court. Stavis believed his small team could be steamrolled by the legal talent Marcos representatives had organized. He also believed that a judge who knew the world was watching might think twice about summarily denying a preliminary injunction. Instead of conducting discovery proceedings in a law office, Stavis asked that they be held in a courtroom. This would open the case to the press.

The district court refused to lift the restraining order. On appeal, the Circuit Court upheld the order. The Supreme Court denied *certiorari*, that is, it refused to place the case on its docket in an expedited fashion; the defendants would have to prove the Marcos properties hadn't been bought with money stolen from the Philippine people. "We considered this a major victory," says Perkins.

It hadn't been easy. Shapiro says the case "consumed Mort for two years." Perkins says the problems were compounded "by the layers of manipulation" the properties had undergone over the years to conceal their true ownership. A man named Bernstein put himself forward as the owner.

"We had to prove that Bernstein was operating as Marcos's agent. Going through this maze took a lot of work. We had to find evidence of all the transfers of money and of title. It was very complex."

A second New York case involved art and jewelry held in the name of no fewer than twenty-three corporations. Armies of attorneys from eleven major law firms bombarded the Center with paper. It became clear that its original mission was over. The cases would continue, but their complexities and hordes of opposing attorneys put them beyond the CCR's capacity.

Stavis arranged for a Newark law firm to take over and to charge the Philippine government a fee substantially below its customary rate. The Center took satisfaction in the role it played. It established, it said, "that dictators cannot use this country as a protected repository for ill-gotten gains, because our courts will entertain the claims of their victims."

An interesting sidebar took place in the course of these events. *The New York Times* saw fit to remind Cory Aquino, Marcos's successor, about a strict rule of the road she was embarking on: no left turn. In a three-column story, *The Times* gave prominence to "critics" who complained that President Aquino's emissaries had hired leftists to represent the republic's legal interests in the United States.

An editorial in *The Nation* on June 14, 1986, took on *The Times*. It said the Center's relationship with the Aquino government was very likely strong enough to withstand the newspaper's "assassination attempt." It pointed out, however, that the episode drew attention to the "fragility" of U.S. support for the Philippine revolution if it was so rash as to show signs of independence from State Department policy. "The CCR is a symbol of opposition to most of that policy's manifestations, and those who associate themselves with the Center have been warned to watch their step."

Severina Rivera acknowledged her own hesitation when she first approached the Center on behalf of her government. For a different reason, however. She says she wasn't sure that property stolen from her countrymen would be considered a civil rights issue. "I was very wrong in thinking the Center was not as politically astute as that." She calls her government's choice of lawyers "impeccable."

Paul v. Avril

General Prosper Avril is a former Haitian dictator. He seized his country's presidency in a coup in 1988 and promptly suspended all constitutional guarantees. Evans Paul is one of six men arrested by Avril's troops for the crime of leading a movement in Haiti for democratic reform. While in custody, the dissidents were beaten and tortured. The National Coalition for Haitian Refugees asked the CCR if it could help. Utilizing the principle established by *Filártiga*, the CCR sued Avril.

The case was brought in the U.S. District Court of the Southern District of Florida in February 1991. It charged that the plaintiffs were deprived of certain specified human rights and sought damages. The general decamped. His lawyers argued that the case should be dismissed. After hearing arguments, the court ordered Avril to return to Florida to stand trial. He failed to appear.

Center attorneys moved in November 1993 for a default judgment. The magistrate ruled the following February that the defendant was guilty of human rights violations. In June 1994, damages were set at $41 million. Although the money was never paid, the Center hailed the decision as "the first in which any Haitian dictator or member of the military has ever been held responsible to any court of law anywhere for human rights abuses . . ."

Doe v. Karadžić

Dr. Radovan Karadžić was the ultranationalist self-proclaimed leader of the Serbs during the 1992–95 war in Bosnia. Serb forces laid siege to and largely destroyed the city of Sarajevo. Eight thousand Muslim Bosnians were slain at Srebenica. Karadžić's responsibility for both actions is the basis for charges brought by the United Nations' war crimes tribunal at The Hague where he is being tried. It is estimated the trial could continue until 2013.

But it was in 1993, when Karadžić was in the United States to press Serbia's cause at the United Nations and raise money for the Serbian war chest, that the Center made its move. Representing a group of Jane and John Does, and invoking the Alien Tort Statute, it brought suit against Karadžić, charging him with genocide, war crimes, and crimes against humanity. Most of the Jane Does sued on behalf of "deceased husbands." One of the John Does sued on behalf of his "infant son."

The judge in the federal district court dismissed the action on the grounds that Karadžić hadn't been a governmental official when the alleged crimes took place, and "acts committed by non-state actors do not violate the law of nations." The verdict was appealed.

"We do not agree," the 2nd District Court of Appeals wrote, "that the law of nations, as understood in the modern era, confines itself to state action. Instead, we hold that certain forms of conduct violate the law of nations whether undertaken by those acting under the auspices of a state or only as private individuals." By extending the reach of the ATS to include private citizens, the impact of the ruling has been significant.

The appeals court ordered *Karadžić* back to the circuit court for a rehearing. Ultimately, the plaintiffs were awarded $4.5 billion in restitution.

John Doe I, et al. v. Unocal Corp., et al.

This case may be said to have drawn breath from *Karadžić*. The Unocal oil company joined with its partners, the French company Total S.A. and the government of Burma, to build a natural gas pipeline in southern Burma. Burmese activists became aware in the early 1990s that laborers on the project were being badly abused, mostly by members of the Burmese army.

"We were contacted," says Jennifer Green, a former Center staff attorney, "mostly because of our human rights line of cases." Green and her colleague Beth Stephens wrote Unocal a threat-to-sue letter. It was ignored. Other lawyers were recruited including a team from EarthRights International.

The suit was brought in 1996 in the name of thirteen Burmese villagers. Unocal was charged with murder, torture, rape, forced labor, battery, and forced relocation. Green says the company used the standard defense that it wasn't complicit. It further claimed that corporations were not non-state actors as defined by *Karadžić*. Attorney

General John Ashcroft filed an *amicus* brief supporting the company's claim.

After many decisions had gone against the plaintiffs, the United States District Court, central district of California, ruled in 2005: "[T]hese allegations are sufficient to support subject-matter jurisdiction under the ATCA." This meant that Unocal's contention, supported by the attorney general, that it was beyond the reach of the Alien Tort Claims Act failed. The company settled for an undisclosed amount.

Unocal "built on the legacy of *Karadžić* to provide a new source of law," says Judith Brown Chomsky, a lawyer on the case. Until *Unocal* it was uncertain whether or not corporations were subject to the same limitations the Alien Torts Statute placed on government functionaries and non-state actors. Corporations ever since have had to be mindful not only of their own comportment, but that of the companies and governments with whom they do business.

Dellums v. Meese

This is perhaps as good an example as any of the readiness of CCR operatives to be no less presumptuous than they are innovative. In 1983, the organization tried to use the law to put an end to U.S. intervention in Central America. A suit was brought to constrain Attorney General Meese to investigate the president. The action claimed the administration, in supporting efforts by a rebel military force to overthrow the government of Nicaragua, was interfering in the affairs of a friendly nation.

That's a violation of the Neutrality Acts adopted by Congress in the 1930s. Plaintiffs were Ron Dellums, a congressman from California; Eleanor Ginsberg, an American from Florida; and Dr. Myrna Cunningham, a Nicaraguan who had suffered wounds in a rebel raid.

The Justice Department tried to brush the CCR aside. The Neutrality Acts, it asserted, apply to individual citizens not high officials. A federal district court magistrate ordered the attorney general either to conduct the investigation or appoint a special prosecutor.

Attorney General Meese appealed. The appeals court took no action for two and a half years. Meantime, some Democratic members of the House Judiciary Committee joined in a request for a special prosecutor to look into the Center's charges. The court ruled in favor of Meese. The plaintiffs, it said, had no standing to make their demand on the attorney general. The Judiciary Committee renewed its request for a special prosecutor. Meese yielded to the pressure in December 1986. He named a special prosecutor, making the legal action no longer necessary.

GOVERNMENT MISCONDUCT

United States v. McSurely
McSurely v. McClellan, et al.

The cases involving Alan and Margaret McSurely are among the CCR's most protracted. The first began in 1967, only months after the organization's birth. A final determination wasn't reached until 1985 in the first case and 1986 in the second action.

The McSurelys had moved to Kentucky to work for the civil rights group, Southern Conference Education Fund

(SCEF). Their assignment was to get poor people to come together to challenge the way local coal companies dominated the region. Their house was raided by local authorities, and they were arrested and charged with violating Kentucky's anti-sedition statute. Their books and documents were confiscated as evidence. Kinoy, Kunstler, and Stavis came to the aid of a local lawyer, Dan Jack Combs.

A CCR organizing principle calls for aggressiveness: the attorneys attacked. A civil action was filed in federal court to have the state's anti-sedition statute declared unconstitutional. The court struck down the statute and ordered state authorities to return the McSurelys' books and papers. Some two hundred documents, however, had been allowed to pass into the hands of the United States Senate's Subcommittee on Government Operations. The committee chairman was John McClellan, a stern Cold Warrior from Arkansas.

In 1968, the McSurelys, represented principally by Stavis, sued McClellan, some of his staff, and the Kentucky prosecutor. The defendants had illegally seized, searched, and distributed the plaintiffs' documents and ought to be held accountable, the suit claimed. It asked a civil court to assess damages.

Meanwhile, the subcommittee was pressing its own attack on the McSurelys. Based on information it had extracted from the documents, it subpoenaed all of the McSurelys' papers. They refused to comply and were charged with contempt of Congress, tried, and convicted.

Five years after the original raid on the McSurelys' home, the United States Court of Appeals in Washington reversed the convictions. The seizure of their books and papers in Kentucky, the court ruled, had violated prohibitions on just such seizures as laid down in the Fourth Amendment. The subsequent subpoena in Washington was therefore illegal.

The civil suit against McClellan and the others continued. In 1975, the defendants were held to be immune from prosecution, under the Constitution's speech and debate clause. The Center's petition for a rehearing was granted. In 1976, the court reversed its ruling of the previous year. The government appealed to the Supreme Court.

Stavis argued that the framers of the Constitution never intended to grant so much immunity to members of Congress that they were free to probe into the private affairs of citizens. Some years later, he would tell a gathering of the National Lawyers Guild that the government's lawyer countered by insisting that the immunity was absolute. "A justice asked him, 'Burglary, too?'" The lawyer held firm. "'What about murder?' His answer was the same. The most that he could yield was to admit to the Court that his answer was 'intuitively unattractive.' It was great for our side; there was little that we had to say after that." The justices agreed and sustained the decision of the lower court. The way was finally clear for the McSurelys' suit to go to trial.

After four years of discovery and preparation, the suit was tried in five weeks in 1982. A jury determined that McClellan had conspired with his aides and with Kentucky law enforcement officials to deprive the McSurelys of rights guaranteed by the Constitution. They were awarded $1.6 million in compensatory and punitive damages.

The defendants appealed. Kentucky settled while the case was still pending. The estate of Senator McClellan argued and lost its appeal in 1984. In 1986, nineteen years after the initial raid, the Senate adopted a resolution to pay the money awarded to the McSurelys.

Dallas CISPES v. FBI

In 1975, Frank Church's Senate Select Intelligence Committee had uncovered COINTELPRO, the FBI's program for spying on Americans who had aroused Director Hoover's widespread suspicions. Under the program, more than twenty-three hundred disruptive actions had been conducted by the FBI against groups it considered subversive. The committee's sensational revelations shattered the bureau's untouchable reputation. Both chambers of Congress named committees and put in place new operational guidelines to make sure the agency would never again exceed its mandate.

1988. The Dallas office of the Committee in Solidarity with the People of El Salvador (CISPES) asks the Center to help it obtain relief from FBI surveillance and harassment. The Center makes inquiries. The FBI stonewalls. The Center files a suit under the Freedom of Information Act. The Justice Department is forced to release its CISPES files.

An example of what's in these files is a communiqué, sent by the FBI's Milwaukee office, which says it's "imperative at this time to formulate some plan of attack against CISPES and specifically against individuals who defiantly display their contempt for the U.S. government by making speeches and propagandizing their cause. . . ." Other reports from agency offices around the country are in a similar vein. "Despite frequent deletions," reports *The Washington Post*, "the voluminous files indicate that the FBI devoted many thousands of hours to surveillance and undercover work, much aimed at church-related activities and college campuses." *Time* notes that the files "show that the investigation eventually touched more than 160 organizations, including the Southern Christian Leadership Conference, the Maryknoll Sisters and the United Auto Workers." Philip Shenon, writing in *The New York Times*, quotes a Justice Department official: "In the end, it was a huge waste of time and money, and it has left egg all over the Bureau's face."

In a public statement, the FBI says it is "sensitive to the constitutional rights of the American public, and the bureau has no interest in interfering with the exercise of these rights." Unpersuaded, several congressional investigating committees request the pleasure of the company of FBI Director William Sessions.

The *Los Angeles Times* writes, "Sessions' rough treatment was very rare for FBI directors. . . ." The article says a committee member told Sessions, "It looks like the honeymoon is over." Sessions is forced to admit the bureau erred badly in its CISPES surveillance. The Senate Intelligence Committee calls on the FBI to purge its files of materials gathered in the course of the investigation. By its intervention, the CCR freed Dallas CISPES from the burden of FBI scrutiny.

United States v. Briggs, et al. ("The Gainesville Eight Conspiracy Case")

A CCR *Docket Report* calls 1973 "in many ways the year of Gainesville at the Center." Perhaps no other case has consumed in one brief period so many of the organization's resources.

The war in Vietnam dominated political activity in the election year 1972. Richard Nixon, running for reelection, could no longer afford to ignore the antiwar movement's expanding ability to mobilize large numbers of demonstrators. An especially effective arm of the movement was the

Vietnam Veterans Against the War (VVAW). Nixon's Justice Department brought indictments in 1972 against seven leaders of the group plus one supporter. They were charged with violating the same statute as the Chicago Conspiracy defendants four years earlier: conspiracy to cross state lines to incite a riot. The parallel is closer still. The riot, according to the government, was to take place at the Republican National Convention in Miami. Peace activists and Center attorneys drew the conclusion that the move to label the VVAW a "violent extremist group" was an attempt to discredit the entire peace movement.

In May 1973, almost a year after the VVAW indictments were issued, a more Machiavellian explanation emerged. The Watergate trials were under way. James McCord, one of those involved in the Watergate break-in, revealed part of the defense strategy. A claim was to be made that the break-in was driven by the justifiable need of preventing violence at the upcoming Republican National Convention. It immediately became the conviction in the "Gainesville Eight" defense camp that to make the claim stick, Nixon and his cohort needed names and faces to attach to this putatively imminent threat to the peace. Enter the VVAW.

The trial was held in Gainesville, Florida, where the original plot was alleged to have been hatched. The government relied heavily on testimony by undercover agents and informers. Three of the latter held leadership positions in the VVAW. When it came time to present its case, the defense called a single technical witness, then rested.

The jury took less than four hours to acquit all defendants on all charges. The *Docket Report* for 1973–74 refers to the drain the case took on the Center's limited time, energy, and resources. "It is in precisely this way that the government ends up the victor, though its case is repudiated and its victims set free."

The heavy toll notwithstanding, the CCR went on to represent some of the defendants in a civil action, *Briggs et al. v. Goodwin et al.*, brought against Justice Department attorney Guy Goodwin and three other government employees. The trial had disclosed that one witness before the grand jury that issued the original indictments had been an informer for the government. Goodwin had given sworn testimony to the contrary.

A year-long discovery process yielded FBI documents establishing that the government had access to strategies developed by defense attorneys in private discussions with the accused. The veterans asked in their suit for the appointment of a special prosecutor to take criminal action against the government's agents. They further asked for reimbursement of their legal expenses and compensatory damages for themselves.

The suit failed and was appealed. In confirming the lower court, the Court of Appeals ruled in 1984 that prosecutors are immune. They can't be sued for their conduct in a trial. At the same time, the opinion noted the "deep concern." The judges found it "troubling that our system of justice, which rests so fundamentally on the consent of the governed, offers such inadequate remedies for official violations of individuals' constitutional rights." For the CCR it was a bitter loss—and a victory at once moral and Pyrrhic.

Horman v. Kissinger

Many know about Charles Horman through the book *Missing* or through the motion picture that was based on it. Few know of the CCR's role.

Horman was a young American living in Chile in 1973 when a military coup overthrew the government of President Salvador Allende. Along with thousands of Chileans, Charles was rounded up by soldiers under the command of the new ruling junta, held secretly, and possibly tortured before being put to death. The coup conformed to vigorous anti-leftist policies being pressed in the region by Richard Nixon's State Department. The American embassy in Santiago withheld what it knew about Horman's fate from his family. One of the things it knew was the reason Horman was killed: he'd learned some of the story of the part the U.S. government had played in the overthrow of Allende.

For four years, Horman's parents tried to find out what happened to their son. At last they asked the Center for help and told a news conference they hoped to find a way to expose Washington's complicity in their son's death. "The law," said Horman's mother, "does not say that Charles is so unimportant that he can be murdered with the consent of our government. We are making this final appeal to law because we believe in law . . ."

A suit was brought against Henry Kissinger and former embassy and military officials representing U.S. interests in Chile at the time of the coup. The complaint alleged that Kissinger helped plot the coup in his role as Special Assistant for National Security Affairs. It asked for a judgment of $4,540,000 in punitive and compensatory damages. It further asked the court to order the government to tell the

Horman family everything it knew about the circumstances of Charles's death.

A U.S. district court dismissed charges against two of the defendants on a technicality in 1980. It subsequently refused to order witnesses stationed abroad brought to the United States to be deposed. And finally the court ruled that the government couldn't be compelled to reveal anything it claimed to be secret. Under these circumstances, the Hormans concluded that the law, for all their belief in it, couldn't help them.

Nancy Stearns had taken a leading role in the case. "It was devastating," she said, "not to be able to do for the Horman family what we wanted to do." She took consolation from knowing the case helped publicize the United States government's shameful role in the tragic events in Chile.

United States v. United States District Court

This wiretap case first began in 1971. It grew out of a conspiracy charge. In the trial, the government admitted tapping the defendant's telephone without a warrant. No warrant was required, it claimed, because the attorney general had authorized the surveillance in keeping with his responsibility for national security. A district court rejected the claim. There can, it held, be no exception to the Fourth Amendment's warrant requirement.

The issue was joined in the Supreme Court on February 24, 1972. Arthur Kinoy was opposed by Robert Mardian, who would soon have his fifteen minutes of notoriety as a figure in the Watergate rogues' gallery. In *Rights On Trial*, his autobiography, Kinoy said Mardian was asking the Court to bestow on the executive branch absolute power to suspend the Constitution. "It was," he wrote, "one of the most dangerous moments in the long history of the Supreme Court."

On June 19, 1972, ruling eight to nothing, the Court confirmed the finding of the lower court, which declared warrantless wiretaps unconstitutional. The Center proclaimed it "one of the most significant victories" in its history. But, as subsequent developments disclosed, the government has resumed the use of warrantless wiretaps under the cover of its war on terror.

Bullfrog Films v. Wick

Despite its obscurity, this case has profound significance. It forced a federal agency (and by extension, other agencies of government) to curb its bureaucratic instinct for political meddling.

The United States Information Agency (USIA) issues "certificates of educational character" to relevant documentary films. A film granted a certificate is exempt, by international treaty, from customs duties. In the impoverished world of documentary filmmaking, a filmmaker, forced to pay the duties, often has to pass up chances at overseas distribution.

The CCR filed a suit in 1985 in federal district court on behalf of several makers of documentaries. The suit contended the USIA was basing some of its decisions to withhold certificates on political considerations. Films that were denied certificates, the suit alleged, were often ones somebody in the agency didn't think ought to be seen, especially outside the country. It charged the plaintiffs' constitutional right to free expression was being violated by arbitrary decisions based on USIA regulations. The court agreed.

The USIA appealed to the Ninth Circuit Court of Appeals in 1988. A ruling affirming the district court held that the agency's regulations gave it "a virtual license to censor." The agency rewrote its regulations. In 1988, the district court held that the new regulations were still too restrictive. It ordered the USIA to issue educational certificates to the plaintiffs.

American-Arab Anti-Discrimination Committee v. Reno ("The Los Angeles Eight")

Seven Palestinians and a Kenyan were arrested in Los Angeles in 1987 and held without bail to await deportation. When they asked what they had done, they were told the Immigration and Naturalization Service (INS) had reason to believe they were "affiliated" with the Popular Front for the Liberation of Palestine (PFLP).

The authorities refused to disclose any evidence. They held that the alleged affiliation meant the accused supported a terrorist organization and so, under certain provisions of the McCarran-Walter Immigration Act, were subject to deportation.

In 1989, a federal district court declared the relevant provisions of the immigration act unconstitutional. Congress responded by repealing the offending provisions and writing a new law that makes "terrorist activity" a deportable offense.

The FBI reported the results of a long investigation of the Los Angeles Eight (LA8): They had committed no crime.

Nevertheless, the INS continued its action against them under cover of the new law.

In 1991, attorneys from the CCR, the National Lawyers Guild, and the ACLU initiated their own action. The suit charged that by refusing to disclose its evidence against the aliens, the INS was violating their right to due process. It also claimed that the LA8 were being selectively prosecuted; other non-citizen residents openly supported groups out of favor in Washington without risking deportation.

The district court, in 1994, issued two preliminary injunctions against the INS. One barred further deportation proceedings against six of the plaintiffs on selective prosecution grounds. The second held that the INS could not use secret information to deny permanent resident status to the two who had applied for it. The ruling made clear that association with the PFLP is protected by the First Amendment. The Justice Department appealed.

Twelve leading constitutional scholars filed an *amicus* brief. The Court of Appeals for the Ninth Circuit, in 1995, affirmed that non-citizens have the same rights as citizens to associate freely and to have access to evidence being used against them.

The court did not order all charges dropped against the last two of the LA8 until February 2007, almost twenty years after the effort to deport them began.

Daniels et al. v. City of New York et al.

A group of citizens approached the CCR in 1999 to ask if anything could be done to curtail the practice by New York City police officers of stopping and searching black and Latino men without apparent cause. The Center brought a class action in the United States District Court for the Southern District of New York charging the city's police with conducting searches in violation of the Constitution's Fourth Amendment. Apart from seeking damages for the plaintiffs, the suit demanded that the police restrict the activities of its Street Crime Unit (SCU), given the unit's central role in the stop-and-frisks. The police argued that the tactic was evenhanded in the way it was carried out and that it was a vital component of the department's crime control effort. Center lawyers produced statistics showing that searches correlated incontestably with skin color and that relatively few of the stop-and-frisks resulted in arrests.

Following the judge's denial of the city's motion to dismiss the action, the police department disbanded the SCU. Whatever the causal connection between the two events may or may not have been, the plaintiffs had reason to celebrate achieving one of their goals. The essence of the other goal was won in September of 2003 when the city settled the suit. The far-reaching terms of the settlement agreement were designed to, on the one hand, make police officers and their superiors conform to Fourth Amendment restrictions on searches and seizures, and, on the other hand, to constrain the city to conduct workshops and classroom sessions to educate neighborhood groups and school kids about their civil rights. The agreement's impact on other police departments was widespread and profound. Over time, in New York City, it came to be honored largely in the breach, so much so that the Center was forced once more to take the city to court.

ATTACKS ON DISSENT

United States of America v. Dellinger et al.

In the tumultuous 1960s, the peace movement staged many actions designed to focus the public's attention on the movement's reasons for opposing the war in Vietnam. Perhaps the most successful was one that took over and held captive for nearly half a year an event staged by the perpetrators of that same war: the trial of the "Chicago Seven."

Eight antiwar activists had been charged with conspiring to travel interstate with the intent of rioting. (Bobby Seale, one of the original accused, was severed from the case and later tried for contempt but never on the substantive charges.) For five months at the end of 1969 and the beginning of 1970, the trial gave the peace movement a national forum.

There was no question that the defendants had helped organize thousands of protesters who went to Chicago in the summer of 1968 to demonstrate against the war at the Democratic National Convention. At issue was whether their activities constituted conspiracy within the meaning of the federal statute.

The CCR's William Kunstler, along with activist attorney Leonard Weinglass, was in charge of the defense. In *My Life as a Radical Lawyer*, Kunstler said he and Weinglass resorted to a unique defense. "Rather than defending the clients, we decided to put the government on trial." They ridiculed the prosecution and succeeded in turning the trial into political theater.

"Judge (Julius) Hoffman was an after dinner speaker on the borscht circuit," Weinglass told me. "He was a jokester. He was playing straight man. Bobby Seale, before he was in the Panthers, in Texas was a standup comedian. Bill Kunstler was an actor (while in the army, he'd had a part in a play). So you had these three main personalities with a sense of timing and a sense of drama and a sense of flare interacting in this political climate. It was an historic perfect storm."

The accused, the judge, the lawyers became national celebrities. From Boston to Barrow, the trial was the smash hit of the season. The men in the dock succeeded, perhaps more than even they could have imagined, in forcing the public to be aware of their cause.

All defendants were acquitted of conspiracy. Five were convicted of intending to organize, promote, and incite to riot. They drew the maximum sentence: five years and $5,000 each.

That left the matter of the many contempt citations Judge Hoffman issued during a trial stinting in decorum but lavish with injudicious remarks. Weinglass says the judge "would instruct Bill and me to control our clients, and Bill took the position, which I agreed with, that we would be violating our role if we would be part of the marshal force in the courtroom." It wasn't their function as attorneys, Weinglass says they repeatedly told the court, to control their clients. Kunstler alone was cited twenty-four times. All citations were ultimately reduced to ten convictions.

Arthur Kinoy led the team that successfully appealed the criminal convictions. Morton Stavis won reversals of all contempt convictions. Kunstler was retried and convicted on two counts. He was sentenced to no jail time, and the Bar Association took no action against him.

Texas v. Johnson

In 1984, Gregory Lee Johnson was arrested in Dallas for violating a Texas statute that prohibits "desecration of a venerated object." The object in this instance was an American flag. It was set on fire outside the 1984 Republican National Convention as part of a protest against Reagan administration policies. Johnson was convicted and sentenced to pay a fine of $2,000 and to spend a year in jail. The Texas Court of Criminal Appeals overturned the conviction. The state's desecration statute, it ruled, was unconstitutional when its use clashed with the First Amendment as it did in *Johnson.* Texas appealed to the United States Supreme Court. The Court accepted the case in 1988.

Johnson asked the CCR to represent him before the Supreme Court. The CCR agreed. The risk was great. A victory would extend the reference to "speech" in the First Amendment to symbolic speech, that is to say, ideas conveyed by non-verbal means. Defeat would place a burdensome restriction on what constitutes speech in an era when the use of image in communication is growing.

By a five-to-four decision, the Supreme Court upheld the ruling of the Texas Appeals Court. Desecrating a flag, it ruled, is a protected form of speech.

Johnson led to a wide and ultimately futile demand for amending the Constitution. William Kunstler, who argued the case, wrote in 1989 that he was "astonished by the vehemence of the reaction" to the Court's decision, noting that every time "we have been stampeded into violating the human rights of our citizens . . . we have belatedly come to regret it."

Soto v. Romero Barcelo ("Cerro Maravilla")

Cerro Maravilla is a mountain in central Puerto Rico. It's the site of many of the island's communication towers. It's also the place where, in 1978, two young Puerto Rican independence activists were gunned down in a police ambush. The police said the two planned to sabotage the towers. The families of the victims sued Governor Romero Barcelo for depriving the youths of their civil rights. Barcelo was head of a statehood coalition. According to the suit, the coalition staged the ambush to discredit the independence movement.

CCR attorneys worked with Puerto Rican groups to press the plaintiffs' claim. Despite the governor's attempt to dismiss the case as politically inspired, it wouldn't go away. By 1983, the government could no longer ignore the fallout. The Puerto Rican Senate launched an investigation into the Cerro Maravilla incident, complete with daily television coverage.

Federal charges of perjury and obstruction of justice were subsequently brought against ten policemen. All were convicted. The civil rights suit was settled in 1984 for an undisclosed but "substantial" sum. An additional significance of the case is the role it played in persuading the Center to become increasingly active in movement activities in Puerto Rico.

United States v. Peltier

Two federal agents were shot and killed on South Dakota's Pine Ridge Indian Reservation in 1975. Leonard Peltier was convicted of murder in connection with the event two years later. Peltier was a leader in the American Indian Movement, an organization formed to protect and advance the rights of Native Americans.

The case has drawn worldwide attention. Those who have filed friend of the court briefs on Peltier's behalf include scores of members of Congress, the Association of Criminal Defense Lawyers, and California Attorneys for Criminal Justice. Among religious leaders, Archbishop Desmond Tutu, the Reverend Jesse Jackson, and the Archbishop of Canterbury have raised urgent questions about the possibility that Peltier is a victim of justice miscarried.

William Kunstler, aided by CCR cooperating attorneys, pressed an appeal to the Eighth Circuit Court of Appeals. Asserting in its decision that at Peltier's trial the FBI withheld evidence that "cast a strong doubt on the government's case," the court nevertheless denied the appeal and refused to grant Peltier a new trial.

The Supreme Court has also backed away from constraining the FBI to subject its handling of the Peltier case to the scrutiny of another judge and another, perhaps less inflamed, jury. In *My Life as a Radical Lawyer*, his autobiography, Kunstler calls Peltier "an all-American political prisoner." He writes that he has "no doubt that at some point, sooner, I hope, rather than later, Leonard Peltier, will gain his freedom." That day has not yet come.

Crockett v. Reagan
Sanchez-Espinoza v. Reagan
United States v. Maria del Scorro Pardo de Aguilar
American Baptist Churches v. Thornburgh
(*"Thornburgh"*)

The movement that commanded more of the Center's attention than any other in the 1980s involved a struggle in their backyard most Americans knew or cared little about: the wars in Central America.

In 1973, Congress passed the War Powers Resolution, 50 U.S.C. s 1541. It required the president to consult with Congress before "introducing United States armed forces into hostilities." U.S. president Ronald Reagan ignored the resolution, using military advisors in El Salvador and sending troops to Grenada, neither time consulting with Congress. *Crockett v. Reagan* was the first of four challenges under the War Powers Resolution. The Center represented George Crockett, a member of Congress. His suit succeeded only to the degree that it established that a court could order the president not to engage military forces without congressional consent.

Sanchez-Espinoza v. Reagan was an ATS case brought on behalf of victims of the so-called "contras" or counter-revolutionaries in Nicaragua, who were receiving large quantities of covert financial and material support from the United States government. The case was a major CCR effort, requiring frequent trips to Nicaragua, some of them not without personal risk. The Center built a nationwide media campaign around the case, exposing the government's involvement in Nicaragua even though the legal action failed.

The *del Scorro Pardo* case involved Federal indictments against priests, nuns, a minister, and volunteers. They were accused of sheltering and harboring illegal aliens. Refugees around the country were rounded up. Churches had begun sheltering refugees driven out of Guatemala and El Salvador by government oppression. By the end of the 1970s, half a million Central Americans had made their way to this country. The churches said they were providing sanctuary in a venerable tradition of Christianity. To Washington, they were meddlesome intruders in foreign relations: Guatemala and El Salvador, never mind the questionable nature of their human rights records, were reliable Cold War allies.

The trial in Tucson took seven months. The judge sided with the prosecution's claim that it was a "simple alien smuggling" case and blocked defense efforts to raise the issues of sanctuary or refuge from oppression. Guilty verdicts drew sentences of probation. Sanctuary movement leaders claimed the publicity the trial attracted gave it a victory.

In the *Thornburgh* case (Attorney General Richard Thornburgh), the Center brought suit on behalf of eight religious organizations to force the government to grant asylum to Central American refugees and to recognize church sanctuary as a First Amendment right. After years of discovery hearings, the court ruled that churches lack "standing" to sue. Still, the Immigration and Naturalization Service (INS) (now USCIS) agreed to review the claims of many refugees who had been denied asylum.

WOMEN'S RIGHTS

Abramowicz v. Lefkowitz ("*Abramowicz*")

This was one of four consolidated cases that launched an attack in 1972 on the constitutionality of the state of New York's restrictive abortion laws in federal court. The case was unique in two ways. Its argument that a woman has a constitutional right to an abortion had not previously been advanced. Further, it approached the abortion question from the equally uncommon perspective of a woman.

Until *Abramowicz*, a woman's right to an abortion had been pressed in the courts as a doctor's right to practice medicine without interference from the state. Or as a poor woman's right to equal access to medical care. The conventional wisdom had always been that women as women lacked standing. Even if accorded standing, they would appear in court as mere women, not commanding the same respect as professionals.

The Center proposed a radical departure from convention. It would bring the action against the abortion statute in the name of a woman. Not of one woman but of three hundred and fifty of them. And it would invoke constitutional guarantees: the decision to have an abortion involves a woman's right to privacy, to life and liberty, and to equal protection of the laws. Moreover, the suit would charge that the restrictive state law, grounded as it was in scriptural doctrine generally and most particularly in the Roman Catholic ban on abortion, was tantamount to an imposition of an establishment of religion.

The Center's proposal didn't ignite enthusiasm in the women's health movement. Many organizations were sure a suit of such radical design would fail and set terrible precedents. The Center persisted.

Abramowicz became moot when New York legislators changed the law. The new statute, adopted well before *Roe v. Wade* (the CCR would later file an *amicus* brief in *Roe)*, guaranteed abortion as a woman's right. The New York plaintiffs' role in forcing this change was widely recognized, and *Abramowicz* went on to become an organizing tool for women throughout the country.

Ultimately, *Abramowicz* became an example of the CCR's readiness to move other institutions into taking more confrontational, not to mention controversial, stances. Its strategy in bringing such an unorthodox case was to extend the use of tactics developed in earlier years by and for the civil rights movement. That movement generated a view of the courtroom as theater. With women's rights cases, the CCR continued and refined the practice of bringing movements, along with their issues, affirmatively and forcefully into the theater of the courtroom.

Klein v. Nassau County Medical Center
McRae v. Califano (Harris v. McRae)

Foes of abortion struck back against New York's new, liberalized law. By restricting access to Medicaid reimbursement, it denied poor women the freedom to terminate an unwanted pregnancy. The state's commissioner of social services issued a regulation that virtually eliminated Medicaid payments for "elective" abortions.

In 1972, *Klein* challenged the restriction in federal court. It contended that Medicaid patients were entitled to medical services for abortion no less than they are to those for childbirth. The court agreed. The commissioner was enjoined against enforcing the regulation. However, the injunction was vacated by the Supreme Court in 1977. Pressure generated by *Klein* and similar legal actions then resulted in a new administrative directive in New York. It broadened the definition of "medically necessary" abortions.

Congress got into the act the same year. An amendment to an appropriations bill placed new limitations on federal matching funds. Only abortions performed to save the woman's life would henceforth be paid for with money from the federal government.

McRae was brought later that year as a challenge to the federal restrictions. It raised the question of poor women's right to equal protection. It also raised the most significant church/state issue to go before a court of law since the Scopes "Monkey Trial."

Evidence was presented that the Roman Catholic Church did not limit its efforts to deny women the right to choose to delivering doctrinal tocsins from the pulpit. Instead, it organized demonstrations, it lobbied, and it raised money, all to advance its campaign against abortion. The role of the Church, in short, was said to be openly political, and the suit charged that Congress had made a law respecting an establishment of religion.

Under the rubric of *Harris v. McRae*, the issues were eventually argued before the Supreme Court. The court, in 1980, ruled that the government could exclude abortion when it provided funds for health care. The setback moved the legal battle to the states.

State of Washington v. Wanrow

Yvonne Wanrow had been convicted of murder in Spokane, Washington, in 1973. She argued in her defense that the victim, a known child molester, had attacked her son. She claimed the right of self-defense and the right to defend her child. She was sentenced to twenty years.

Wanrow is a Colville Native American. After her conviction, the American Indian Movement put her in touch with William Kunstler, well known to AIM activists through his work at Wounded Knee. Kunstler referred Wanrow to the CCR.

Elizabeth Schneider led a team of women attorneys from the Center. They argued to the Washington Supreme Court that the trial judge erred when he failed to direct the jury to fully consider the circumstances that led Wanrow to claim she was defending herself and her child when she pulled the trigger. The justices agreed and ordered the state to retry Wanrow. The ruling was tailored to historic dimensions: for the first time a U.S. court acknowledged the special legal problems that burden women when they and their children are victims of male abusers.

Center lawyers pressed their appeal of Wanrow's conviction by raising objections to the homicide statutes under which she'd been brought to trial. The state retreated, and she was never retried. Ultimately, her sentence was reduced to five years' probation.

IN CONCLUSION

The above cases exemplify how a handful of lawyers and legal workers can use the law, if not to effect social change, to at least nudge the social order in the direction of fairness, equity. The cases graphically illustrate, as well, how extraordinary the dedication to the task has to be. What they demonstrate is a willingness to be aggressive and to persevere, even in the face of years of litigation often ending in defeat in court. Always, the lawyers and the people they represented understood that the legal battles were a step taken toward the broader goal in order to inject them into the public discourse.

CHAPTER 11

Funding

It's 6 o'clock Christmas day. CCR development director Kevi Brannelly is in her office just in case a rescue call comes in. Ten days earlier, the JEHT Foundation announced its assets were wiped out in the 2008 Bernard Madoff debacle; the funding group was closing its doors. A $380,000 hole had abruptly opened in the Center's 2009 budget. Into the same abyss had gone JEHT's half-million pledge toward the Center's next fiscal year.

The phone rings. Brannelly is told the liberal online group MoveOn realizes that many non-profits were affected by Madoff's collapse, and "we wanted to make sure your guys' work doesn't suffer for losing income." Brannelly explains her problem. The caller says MoveOn will do a fundraiser. That's Friday. The appeal goes out Monday on behalf of the Center and several similarly stricken organizations. "So it was a four-day push, four days until the end of the year." Four days before donors would close their books for the year. The Open Society Institute and the Atlantic Foundation match money raised from MoveOn donors. "We got about $300,000, which bought us six or seven months to replace" the JEHT grant.

Until the Guantánamo cases put the CCR into public relations orbit, raising the money required for its operation was a whole other kind of activity.

"You look at their docket and you say, 'My God, is this the Rockefeller Foundation?' It just doesn't strike me as being a viable way to run an organization." Attorney Victor Rabinowitz was just finding the range. The CCR, he charged, is an organization with "stars in its eyes." In evidence he offered the number of programs it had taken on that it couldn't handle given its resources. "They had X dollars, where to do what they wanted to do they'd need 20X."

Center people don't deny projects had to be abandoned when funds ran out, but they have no patience with appeals to prudence. From the beginning, their method of operating has been to call the tune loudly and clearly and figure out later how to pay the piper. Many completed cases, they insist, would never have been undertaken if they had had to be budgeted in advance. The Center has always operated on the theory that you have to do the work to get the money. The Guantánamo cases allow the group to claim nothing if not *quod erat demonstrandum.* The organization's budget in 2003 was $2.7 million. *Rasul,* the Supreme Court's habeas corpus decision, was decided in June of the following year. By '08 the budget was $4.5 million. In '09 it was $5.5 million. The 2010 budget was $7.5 million. There can be no mistaking the connection to the *Rasul* decision. So great now is the group's confidence in its ability to raise money that for the past several years it has passed deficit budgets.

Foundation to individual giving runs about 60 percent/40 percent, with the balance tipping one way, then the other. Brannelly says more than the ratio, it's the spread of grant money that concerns her. "What makes me nervous is when we have a relatively few foundations giving very large grants. So if you lose any one of those . . . " Vincent Warren agrees. He'd like reliance on foundation grants reduced to 30 percent.

Brannelly has a staff of eight to help maintain and nurture the individual donor side of the equation. A donor base of fewer than four thousand annually yields between two and three million dollars. "So we have some really solid amazing major donors," she says. "Unfortunately, they're from a generation that knew how to give—that philanthropic generation, people who are in their sixties and above. We don't see that kind of stay-with-you-through-thick-and-thin in the younger generation." As normal attrition takes its toll, the development staff concentrates on expanding the base of more modest givers. "We have to go out and get the online giver who gives $15 a month," Brannelly says, "because they'll continue to give $15 a month." She believes the key is contact. She's added a comment card to appeal mailings, says she reads each one that comes back. "I don't want anybody to ever think we're so big we forget about the $25 gift." When the cards come in, she and her staff write notes back as often as they can. "That's so important, that relationship, that feeling that they're connected."

One way contact in the New York area is maintained is by holding monthly donor forums for more substantial givers. The site is a conference room at the Center offices.

Lunch is laid on while a staff attorney briefs the group on a noteworthy case.

Occasional forays are undertaken to other cities to meet with major donors. Boston. San Francisco. Seattle. Infrequently, Chicago. Los Angeles ("But," says Brannelly, "that's a challenge"). These missions mostly are undertaken by Warren. A staff lawyer with work in a given area might be diverted to meet with a donor or foundation. Another way donors around the country are kept plugged in is by Development and Education & Outreach working together to organize events that offer people who have given money a chance to come hear about work the CCR is doing.

The Center's has never been a board based on wealth. Since the beginning, people qualified for the board by the strength of their commitment to the CCR's mission. Personal wealth and access to wealth were never requirements. Before raising money was made part of the executive director's job description, board members took responsibility for meeting budget requirements, knowing they could count on chairman Robert Boehm's generosity to meet any shortfall. The Center's board numbers twenty; the New York Public Library's, by way of comparison, sixty.

Brannelly says the current directors have elected to increase the board's involvement in funding their organization, despite several objections from members who make it clear that isn't what they signed up for. It isn't, she says, an easy cultural shift. Nonetheless, it's one that she's convinced is taking place, and that the financial future of the Center is, as a result, more secure.

CHAPTER 12

Docket Report

After so many years of working in the wilderness and walking a financial tightrope, today's CCR is a smoothly running organization, with twenty-odd staff attorneys and legal workers backed by efficient departments for education and outreach, development, public relations, and administration. The group's future is bright with promise, pulsing with ambition.

Having devoted more energy and resources to the Guantánamo Initiative than to any but a few campaigns in its history, the organization is returning to its core mission. It continues to represent GITMO clients, "and will," says Ratner, "for many years, I'm afraid. And our goal is still to dismantle the national security state, especially as it was enhanced by Bush and continued by Obama." State secrecy, preventive detention, military commissions, rendition (the holding of a detainee for the United States government in a foreign prison), and, of course, closing down the detention center at Guantánamo all remain CCR targets.

"This is Obama's Guantánamo now," says executive director Warren. Four attorneys and three legal workers remain attached to the Initiative more or less full-time. The normal legal problems for their clients were compounded when Justice Elena Kagan recused herself for two years on any detainee matter, making the Supreme Court, where the Center has had its only Guantánamo successes, virtually unapproachable for that period. The Initiative remains undeterred. Apart from continuing to pursue the cases of its eleven individual clients, it's actively engaged in finding homes for some of the ninety detainees who have been cleared for release. It is pressing civil actions on behalf of a number of prisoners and their families demanding restitution for mistreatment, including torture, suffered while captives of the United States government.

The Center's core mission remains to work for social change and to make sure that what former legal director Bill Quigley calls society's "non-people" have access to justice. The correspondence of these non-people with race and class is something Center people accept as a given.

How is it expected that interaction with this constituency will be accomplished? How, going forward, can the Center hope to offer access to justice to an immigrant caught in an ICE sweep? To an African American charged with terrorism in connection with his affiliation to an inner-city mosque? "We get hundreds of phone calls," says Vincent Warren, "e-mails from individuals and groups saying can you come help us."

The Center first wants to know if there are others to whom it can refer such pleas. If not, if other organizations are inappropriate or elect to pass, that could mean any such orphaned request might merit closer CCR scrutiny. When it's found that a community group is raising an issue *that's tied to a broader movement* and has encountered legal obstacles, "[T]hat," says Warren, "becomes very attractive to us."

At the same time, the Center isn't waiting for cases to come to it, as it were, over the transom. It is actively trying to foresee problems that may require its services. Having identified a developing problem, it will work with a community group on the ground to test its assumptions. What's the group experiencing? Tapped phones? FBI informants?

Warren is careful to make clear the process doesn't mean the Center is plaintiff hunting. "We have to be able to say, 'Is what we're seeing really happening?'" The object of the exercise is to learn if an issue is going to be one that's likely to command the group's attention. Should it be preparing? It's an example of the tension that has agitated Center lawyers since the beginning, and indeed burdens all left lawyers—the tension between the urge to organize a vanguard and the understanding that their role is to wait to be summoned by a new formation readying itself to press for social change.

What makes the Center's current agenda especially interesting is the disappearance of broad movements such as those that swept it up in its early years. No longer is it able comfortably to define itself as the legal arm of this or that movement. Self-definition thus becomes trickier. What, in 2011, exactly is the Center for Constitutional Rights? Taking the place of movements are communities, less stirring perhaps, less ambitious, but in many instances vital and rich in their potential impact on social change. "It's part of our role to at least understand" the way people are building communities, says Warren, "and to do what we can to support that if legal action is appropriate."

Legal action, as we've seen, is not an invariable component of Center involvement. There are times when its work with a community produces organizing and educational opportunities without any recourse to the courts. It means, says Quigley, "the lawyers who are working on social change have to be in communication and in some sort of relationship with the people who are trying to do it in other forms as well."

An example: Members of a South African housing and land rights movement paid the Center a visit in 2009. Would the CCR send a delegation to South Africa to establish a link to the fight there for housing? The CCR would and did. Firm bonds were formed with movement activists. Moreover, a letter was sent to South Africa's Department of Justice and to the Department of Rural Development and Land Reform expressing concern for human rights abuses.

Social and economic matters have been given central positions on the Center's agenda. Close attention is being paid to housing, hunger, education, and gay rights. Warren says that merely because the framers of the Constitution didn't ordain that people have rights in these areas doesn't mean that the CCR should not be actively finding ways to adapt existing laws.

On the Center's docket, too, is pressing universal jurisdiction litigation to make officials of the George W. Bush administration accountable for human rights violations. Because legal action in the United States is ruled out by laws covering official secrets, the Center has intervened to bring its legal expertise to an investigation by a Spanish court of interrogations conducted under Bush's rules.

The Center doesn't believe the Obama Justice Department has significantly loosened its grip on the extraordinary powers claimed by its Bush predecessors. It is looking, for example, into prisons outside the United States where, Quigley says, "the U.S. will hold people directly or has a wink-and-a-nod relationship with another country that's holding people they don't want to bring to the U.S. but want to interrogate."

The organization wants to do more on gender and race issues, not only domestically but globally. In those areas, it's being asked, says Quigley, "to pitch in on the most wonderful, interesting, challenging issues all the time, and so the question is really trying to line up who can do that work and where the resources will come from."

Quigley says that because the organization is larger than it has ever been, he's concerned that it "can still be agile, can still move rapidly, can the lawyers do a criminal case one day and an international case the next day and then go out on the street and represent people who are marching the day after." He takes a moment to reflect. "I think the organization has a good sense of itself. Nobody knows how to make it all happen. Nobody has a blueprint."

The absence of a blueprint didn't trouble Morton Stavis. Shortly before he died he assessed the CCR's staying power in a changing world and pronounced it unlimited: "The principles which we've tried to develop in the Center, namely aggressive, innovative struggle for human rights and constitutional principles, will survive." When, nearly two decades later, people come asking for the Center's help from as far off as South Africa, there's no question he knew what he was talking about.

Afterword

Americans in 1933 confronted the specter of the Great Depression. The national anthem was E. Y. "Yip" Harburg's "Brother, Can You Spare a Dime?" And yet, in the face of the most complete economic collapse of the modern era, President Franklin Roosevelt was able to assure his countrymen that the only barrier between them and a bright future was their own paralyzing fear.

Three quarters of a century later, Americans have more to fear than fear itself.

The gap dividing rich and poor continues to widen. The world's willing-to-work population exceeds opportunities for gainful employment—by 50 percent in Zambia, 60 percent in Tajikistan, 90 percent in Zimbabwe, 16.5 percent in the United States. Those among us with jobs learn new words—retrenchment, restructuring, downsizing, maquiladora, free trade zone—and we have reason to be afraid.

National governments cede sovereignty to corporations over a planet with ever more people contending for contracting resources. The destruction of ecosystems gathers speed at an alarming rate. Climatologists warn of fast-approaching tipping points after which, if ignored, we confront a future when life on our planet is no longer sustainable. People are afraid for good reason.

Some of us arm ourselves with handguns or assault weapons or an avenging god against fears both real and imagined.

Eyes ever on the main chance, our political leaders encourage fear, direct it to targets of opportunity: terrorists, immigrants, gays and lesbians, those who don't dress, eat, play, worship as "we" do. Having exploited our anxiety, these leaders feel free to arm themselves with Patriot Acts and other instruments of repression, displaying disdain for any constitutional specifications that might be expected to impede their purpose.

So much cynical leadership breeds contempt for politics and its institutions. Whereupon, turning even our contempt to their advantage, politicians offer up government itself as a scapegoat. Once viewed, no matter how uncertainly, as an instrument of collective strength, government is now widely maligned. And no more than by those pleased to style themselves "public servants."

Government, they tell us, is a millstone which, if we're wise, we'll get off our backs. They assure us that with less government we'll pay lower taxes and be subject to fewer regulations. They hope that in our fear we won't ask where, if not to government, will we turn for support for education, for medical care, for aid to dependent children, for occupational safety, protection against product abuse, air and water pollution, public land despoliation, food and drug adulteration.

Ever larger corporations are turned loose to pursue profits without regard not only to local sensibilities but even to national boundaries. If we ask questions about that arrangement, we're told globalization is driven by the ultimate arbiter: the market. And so social responsibility is mothballed for the duration. Working people the world over lose ground.

Even as we dutifully swallow our daily dose of fear and fury, our attention is directed by our leaders to yet other afflictions, grievances for which these same impeachers of government offer a surprising remedy: government. Look to government, they urge, to narrow the gap between church and state, to make criminal the sin of terminating unwanted pregnancies, to restrict voting laws, to combat crime with prisons and law enforcement, to monitor us closely lest there be terrorists among us, to expel immigrants, to deprive people of the same sex of their right to marry.

When jobs and homes and secure futures have vanished or been placed at risk, it makes sense to be both angry and afraid. For a society so assailed, to be beguiled by solutions that further restrict an already limited democracy likewise may seem to make sense, especially when alternative solutions are absent.

The Center for Constitutional Rights was quick to see the danger and to plant itself squarely between an angry, frightened, confused society on the one hand and the United States Constitution and Universal Declaration of Human Rights on the other.

It is, of course, an absurd idea. A non-profit legal and educational organization? Forty-three people, a mere dozen of them lawyers? And yet forty odd years ago no less absurd was a notion that a quartet of upstart public interest lawyers could play key roles in bringing down a venerated system of institutionalized bigotry in the Deep South.

The four are dead. The organization they founded to help them contribute their skills to the black liberation struggle is alive and as well as can be expected given that it had to acknowledge in its annual report at the end of its first decade that its "penchant for difficult cases is sometimes misinterpreted as a legal death wish."

Daunting as were the odds against the Center in the sixties, they're even heavier now. The socialist vision has grown clouded. The dynamic popular movements that sustained the organization from its beginning are everywhere in retreat. Their disintegration was, for a time, threatening to leave it deprived of afflatus.

Then came 9/11 and the resulting assault on the Constitution. The Center responded with its challenge to George W. Bush's war on terrorism, drawing attacks from all sides. Certain of its course and with renewed vitality, the Center persevered. As a consequence, it is stronger and better positioned now for the tough fight against forces engaged in exploiting popular fear and anger.

Times have seldom been worse for the law as a means of bringing about social justice. After eight years of Bush appointments to the federal bench, the courts are particularly unwelcoming. That, say people at the Center for Constitutional Rights, goes with the territory. They opened federal courthouse doors to blacks oppressed by state laws in the South. They aggressively defended opponents of the war in Vietnam. They were in the forefront of developing a legal foundation for the women's movement. They made corporations liable anywhere in the world where they violated the human rights of their employees.

A volunteer to stand in the path of history? It's why journalist Alexander Cockburn styled them "that splendid body of tigerish people." It's what they do.

Index